Korn
Follow The Leader

Laura Shenton

"We already knew we had a cult following, and there was a future that we could shape on our own. It felt like the creative doors got kicked down and we were able to try anything."

- Munky, August 2018

"We were just some kids from Bakersfield — it was some crazy, dream-come-true shit."

- Jonathan Davis, August 2018

Korn
FOLLOW THE LEADER

Laura Shenton

WYMER PUBLISHING
Bedford, England

First published in 2021 by Wymer Publishing
Bedford, England www.wymerpublishing.co.uk Tel: 01234 326691
Wymer Publishing is a trading name of Wymer (UK) Ltd

Copyright © 2021 Laura Shenton / Wymer Publishing.

ISBN: 978-1-912782-68-0 (also available as Kindle eBook).

Edited by Jerry Bloom.

The Author hereby asserts his rights to be identified
as the author of this work in accordance with sections
77 to 78 of the Copyright, Designs & Patents Act 1988.

All rights reserved. No part of this publication may be
reproduced or transmitted in any form or by any means,
electronic or mechanical, including photocopying, or any
information storage and retrieval system, without written
permission from the publisher.

This publication is sold subject to the condition that it shall not,
by way of trade or otherwise, be lent, re-sold, hired out or
otherwise circulated without the publishers' prior consent in any
form of binding or cover other than that in which it is published
and without a similar condition including this condition
being imposed on the subsequent purchaser.

Printed and bound in Great Britain by
CMP, Dorset.

A catalogue record for this book is available from the British Library.

Typeset by Andy Bishop / 1016 Sarpsborg.
Cover design by 1016 Sarpsborg.
Cover photo © Globe Photos/ZUMAPRESS.com (Alamy Stock Photo).

Contents

Preface   7

Chapter One: *Why Follow The Leader?*   9

Chapter Two: *The Making of Follow The Leader*   32

Chapter Three: *Touring And Making An Impact*   63

Chapter Four: *A Legendary Album*   81

A Comprehensive Discography   105

Tour Dates   108

Preface

Considering the musical impact that Korn have made throughout their tenure, there hasn't been that many books written about them. Whilst there are a few biographical and autobiographical accounts out there already, the purpose of this book is to look at the music in detail. In this case, the 1998 album, *Follow The Leader*.

As author of this book, it is my aim to offer an insight into *Follow The Leader* in a way that discusses the music in detail in relation to what Korn's creative process was. I want to offer something factual rather than something that is peppered with my own opinion and interpretation of the music. You won't see statements in the lexicon of "this section is in the key of A and it therefore means X" or "I think this lyric means Y." For of course, the beauty of music is often in the ambiguity; it would be futile to throw a lot of my own opinions out there because it won't add anything to the literature if I do that.

The purpose of this book is to look at *Follow The Leader* in detail; an extent of detail that has been put out there by Korn in terms of what was intended by the album and detail regarding how the album was perceived at the time. As a result, throughout this book you're going to see lots of quotes from vintage articles. I think it's important to corroborate such material as there will probably come a time when it is harder to source.

Some of Korn's legacy, particularly with regard to their earlier days, is surrounded in controversy in terms of the subject matter of Jonathan Davis' lyrics and how the media have responded to them (and indeed Korn's image overall). Then of course, there's the whole sex, drugs and rock and roll stuff on top of that and truthfully, it is understandable as to why many may regard Korn, their music, and their fans as being quite volatile. Objectively, for every small handful of people who consider Korn to be in poor taste, there are millions of fans out there who take them as they are: pioneers of just some damn good music. In writing this book, that's what I want to focus on. However, in the interests of wanting to offer an objective narrative on the music, it is impossible to omit or indeed gloss over controversies where they are relevant to the music.

In the interest of transparency, I have no affiliation with Korn or with any of their associates. This book is based on extensive research and objective commentary.

Throughout this book, I'll refer to all members of Korn by their chosen nicknames, as they have most often presented in interviews:

Jonathan Davis — lead vocals, bagpipes
James "Munky" Shaffer — guitars
Reginald "Fieldy" Arvizu — bass guitar
Brian "Head" Welch — guitars, vocals
David Silveria — drums, percussion

Chapter One
Why Follow The Leader?

Jonathan Davis was quoted of *Follow The Leader* in *Kerrang!* in July 1998; "Our heads were going a hundred miles an hour on finishing this album. It's the most important album of our lives, and the best we've done."

In response to hearing a preview of the album, a journalist advocated; "From the moment 'It's On!' kicks in through the massive speakers with a riff that would dwarf Godzilla, it's obvious that we're not about to be disappointed. 'Dead Bodies Everywhere', 'Got The Life' and the rest all grab hold of your emotions and squeeze out the bad stuff. Korn — You wouldn't want them to organise your wedding. Or indeed, a tipple in your local brewery. But they have almost certainly recorded the finest album of 1998."

When Korn released *Follow The Leader* on 18th August 1998, they already had a strong following of fans and they were already established in their unique sound that had propelled them to success. However, whilst Korn's 1994 eponymous debut album and their 1996 album, *Life Is Peachy*, had already earned them popularity, *Follow The Leader* made the band a household name.

More than fourteen million copies of *Follow The Leader* have been sold to date, making it their most popular album. It spawned the two hit singles, 'Got The Life' and 'Freak On A Leash'. Due to fans requesting it so much, 'Got The Life' was the first video to be officially retired from MTV's *Total Live Request* show. Davis was quoted in *The Fader* in August 2018; "The *Total Request Live* retirement home is because of us. We were the first band to be retired because our video would not get out. It stayed number one and two for so fucking long MTV had to figure something out. I have the plaque on my wall."

Korn - *Follow The Leader*: In-depth

The more the singles were played on MTV, the more Korn's profile, and indeed the intensity of the fanbase increased. Davis was quoted of 'Freak On A Leash' in *The Fader* in August 2018; "Our fans are so fucking rabid — they wouldn't stop calling, they just kept it there. MTV was like, 'Man they have to go away.' Every time we'd be on *Total Request Live* or anything like that, there would be literally thousands of people out there, they'd have to call the fucking police. We had shit tons of bodyguards, cars almost getting tipped over. It was ridiculous, like some Beatles-type shit back then."

He was quoted in *Loudwire* in August 2019; "The huge success of 'Freak On A Leash' and 'Got The Life' freaked the fuck out of us. We went through some wild adjusting periods. Nobody was getting along and we were all going crazy because of all this fame. Before then, we could go out in the crowd and talk to people. All of a sudden I needed a bodyguard everywhere I went. I couldn't go anywhere because people would be rushing me and I never wanted that."

Davis was quoted in *Kerrang!* in March 1998; "Stuff like being on a record company and going to buy a new house. I mean, shit! I used to live in a garage and eat crackers! I've changed so much, it's weird man. It's hard for me. I'm kind of in denial of it. Sometimes I think 'I've got money now. I'm gonna be a chump. I ain't gonna be real no more.' I feel like I've got one foot in the new life an one foot in the old. Maybe I should just fucking accept what I've got and enjoy it!... We've just got more freedom. We've bought cars and shit like that. We've got families. But as people no one's changed at all. We're still as tight as ever."

In a press release for *Follow The Leader*, Davis said of 'Got The Life'; "I'm baggin' on myself in that song. It's about how everything's always handed to me, how I look up to God and say I don't want this anymore. I want something more out of life than all this. And I've got everything I really need, but sometimes I don't like it and I don't know how to explain it. I have to sit through the songs more to actually get into what I write. I really and truly know the meanings of the songs — almost. But it's like I'm haunted by demons that influence my writing. It's a give or take of that. I love being a rock star, I love all that it entails, but I hate all the pressure and all the bullshit's that involved. And I'm asking God, you know, take this away and make me happy. But he's telling me, 'hey, you got the life. You get to see the world, you get to do this, you get to be in a great big band.' My mindset when I was writing the song was that I was really down on everything. I'm sick of this bullshit, all the stress and the pressure. But if it were all gone, I'd be in even more hell."

****

It is argued by some that *Follow The Leader* helped to bring the genre of alternative metal into the mainstream. It was certified platinum in the USA in March 2002 as well as triple platinum in Australia and Canada. As soon as it was released, *Follow The Leader* landed safely at number one on the Billboard 200 chart. 268,000 copies of the album were sold in just the first week. It was advocated in *Total Guitar* in September 1998; "Korn's third album is called *Follow The Leader*, a half joking, half serious comment on their influence over an entire generation of new rockers. Korn's trademark seven-string Ibanez assault, from guitarists Munky and Head, has set a legion of new players in search of manic detuned riffs and atonal solos."

Munky was quoted in the same feature; "Well, you can't help but notice it and it is nice. You know the saying that imitation is the highest form of flattery? It is cool, what can I say? Good luck, maybe. But there is only one Korn... You always try to do something new and different. It has to move forward and you deliver something new but still remain within the established framework. Although a lot of people will say that everything has been done with guitars, but I don't think so... I don't think that the guitar playing depends on technological breakthroughs, but on the imagination of the players. It's possible that a generation of musicians has been busy with innovations in technology, but there are still loads of guitar players in traditional rock bands."

The album gave Korn the perfect platform to expand on their success and to grow bigger than ever. It gave them a platform upon which the Family Values tour was built. The tour helped to boost the careers of other artists: Orgy, Incubus, Limp Bizkit and Rammstein.

It also resulted in rapper Ice Cube being able to engage with a new fanbase.

Fieldy was quoted of the tour in *Kerrang!* in January 1999; "(Ice Cube) was winning over the crowd more than anyone. They loved him! He came out and did 'Children Of The Korn' with us every single night. Another highlight for me was doing 'All In The Family' with the whole of Limp Bizkit. We were on one half of the stage and they were on the other. One band would play their verse, then stop, and the other band would play theirs. It went back and forth, the whole song"

Munky was quoted in *Total Guitar* in September 1998; "We've really got to know each other as players and people, and perhaps matured as musicians. That still doesn't mean we don't have an off show, now and again. We are all human and it happens to everyone."

Fieldy was quoted of the Long Island Coliseum gig of the tour in *Kerrang!* in January 1999; "I remember that as the one night that was bullshit, with security telling kids to sit down. All the other nights were great — there was an open floor and the kids got to go crazy."

The Family Values tour helped to promote *Follow The Leader* and the singles from it. 'Freak On A Leash' won MTV awards for Best Rock Video and Best Editing. It also won a Grammy Award in 2000 for Best Short Form Music Video. Featuring a bullet bolting through the streets in slow motion, the video stayed in the top ten on *Total Request Live* for three months before MTV decided to retire it, as with 'Got The Life', due to the overwhelming number of requests.

Fieldy said to *The Fader* in August 2018; "We don't really fit into this, I don't understand.' It was so mind-boggling, I was just in denial. And then it kept being number one."

Munky was quoted in the same feature; "You couldn't knock that thing off. Not even the Backstreet Boys could knock it off! That's hilarious to me. But that's how music is: diverse."

Head was quoted in *The Fader* in August 2018; "The Video Music Awards were nerve-wracking, man. Everyone in the music business that's hot was there, and we're sitting up in the front, right behind Dr. Dre and Eminem. I remember walking up to the awards, and we ran into Will Smith right away and we were like, 'What's up Big Willy!' I think he had the Wild Wild West thing, and they were calling him Big Willy. He didn't know our names so he was just like 'KORN! HEY WHAT'S UP KORN?' And seeing Tommy Lee — When I was a kid, I would sit there for hours and draw Mötley Crüe — their faces, their costumes, everything. I would listen to them for hours. So for him to give us an award was just so surreal. What a magical night. After the awards, we all went in different directions. My wife and I ended up at one of the after parties — this little dive bar in New York City, invitation-only. We're walking through and look at the bar, and there's Paul McCartney talking to Madonna. I'm just like, okay, that tops the night."

Commercially, things were going fantastically for Korn. Sadly though, the year of 1998 was also tarnished with excess in the form of addiction problems (both the presence of them and the efforts to be free of them). Life on the road was just as exhausting and emotionally challenging as it was beneficial for the band's profile overall. *Follow The Leader* propelled Korn to a new level of fame and of course, that came with difficulties as well as something to be proud of. The release of *Follow The Leader* meant big things for Korn and also for a generation of music fans, many of whom could relate to the angst and emotion portrayed in their heavy sound and dark lyrics. But of course, in the run up to 1998, Korn had been on quite the journey when it came to how they developed their sound and indeed, fanbase. Head was quoted in *Loudwire* in September 2019; "We started in our early twenties. I didn't think we would get as big as we did."

****

Prior to the existence of Korn, there was a band by the name of L.A.P.D. The band was formed in Bakersfield, California in 1989 by Fieldy, Munky and David Silveria. L.A.P.D. were one of thousands of bands on the West Coast who were trying to emulate the funk inspired rock of the Red Hot Chili Peppers with a dash of weirdness inspired by Faith No More. At a time when rock still had a hangover from eighties hair metal, the ground was fertile for creating a blend of sound. When it came to L.A.P.D. — and indeed many bands on the scene at the time — there was a question of "is this really working?"

Korn - *Follow The Leader*: In-depth

Fieldy was quoted in *Kerrang!* in January 1999; "I've kinda blocked L.A.P.D. out. We were trying to be a cross between Faith No More and the Chili Peppers, but we didn't know which way we were going."

Munky had always considered Steve Vai as an influence. This was key in him choosing to embrace the possibilities of what could be done with a seven-string guitar. He was quoted in *Guitarist* in October 1998; "I love Steve Vai, and meeting him, I was just eighteen all over again. But I like him because he plays from the heart. I'm not into all that fast, flashy stuff that he does... When I go back home, I like to chill out and listen to Moorcheeba and Portishead, they're my current favourites. It's not like I get home and put a Slayer album on!... Head and I both play Ibanez seven-strings, the ones Steve Vai designed. I really admire him for doing that, he's always pushing the boundaries of the instrument, and I'm surprised he hasn't had a sixth finger added to his hand by now!... The deal with Ibanez is that we get free guitars. I really had to scrimp and save before that. But I don't know why I'm an endorsee, I'm not even that good! I'm really pleased though as I've been playing the seven-string ever since you could buy it. At first, no one was buying them. Now, Ibanez is selling about five hundred a month."

Munky was ambitious from a young age. He was quoted in *Total Guitar* in September 1998; "I was fourteen. I looked at myself in the mirror holding a guitar and spoke to myself aloud — 'One day I'm gonna make it in the music business.' From that day on, I sat in my room and played guitar. All of my friends would go out, partying, and I'd always refuse because I was really into music. It was more important to me than anything else in the world."

L.A.P.D. fell apart and saw Munky, Fieldy and Silveria head to LA in search of a more aggressive sound. Cue the recruitment of Head for extra guitar power. Head was quoted of L.A.P.D. in *Rolling Stone* in December 2014 as having "waited years for them to get through their stupid funk phase."

Head and Munky began to experiment with the use of pedals and down-tuned riffs in order to acquire a heavier sound. Munky was quoted in the same feature; "We were trying to sound like a DJ had remixed our guitars, y'know, and cutting them up and scratching. That's kind of how that sound was born."

Fieldy: "When I would want to slap my bass, I wanted it to sound like it was being slapped. I didn't want it to sound like a bass; I wanted it to sound like if you slapped a string. I don't even like bass, to tell you the truth — it makes me nauseous."

By this point, the band was called Creep. Heaviness and aggression was the order of the day, so much so that Creep's music was absent of many conventions in rock music; melodic guitar solos and hooks. Artistically, Creep were in a reasonably good position having established a heavy and distinctive sound. However, something was missing. They had no frontman to give their music that spark that was very much missing.

Meanwhile, one Jonathan Davis was contributing his vocal talents to a local funk-metal band called Sexart. Unlike Creep, Davis' musical inspirations were Duran Duran and the musical, *Jesus Christ Superstar*. Choosing to wear eyeliner at school, Davis considers that it wasn't until he heard Pantera's 1992 album, *Vulger Display Of Power*, that he was first exposed to metal.

Creep were very impressed with Davis and wanted him as their frontman. Munky was quoted in *Total Guitar* in September 1998 as he recalled meeting Jonathan Davis; "Head and I went to Bakersfield and went to a bar. This guy came on and started singing. Head and I looked at each other and decided to stay. We had a few more beers and checked him out. It was Jonathan — and we watched the whole set — he was a great frontman. When they finished the show we had a little talk. When he came down to us, it took one song to know that he was the missing element in our music. He completed our sound. Jonathan brought a more aggressive element to the band, emotionally speaking. He opened doors to certain melodies and helped us to expand our musical horizons. He's never been a singer who screamed, he just wants to add something heartfelt."

It was after consulting a psychic that Davis agreed to join Korn. It's crazy to think that if the psychic didn't concur, then there might be no such thing as Korn as we know it! Head was quoted in *Rolling Stone* in December 2014; "When we had this scarecrow, depressed-sounding singer, and we're doing all these noises, it just kind of went together and it made it sound even weirder."

Davis was quoted in *The Independent* in May 2017; "Creep had this weird, funky Alice In Chains vibe going on and this crazy dude called Corey singing for them who sounded exactly like Layne Staley. Their music was really dark, heavy and minor but he made them sound kinda happy. When I tried out, I heard the first note and immediately went for a darker feel; from that very first note I knew we had something special."

As a frontman, Davis didn't fit into any of the plausible rock stereotypes at the time. He wasn't macho, intellectual or clownish. He was very much reflective of his own niche. Davis' act was one built on intense emotion — an over-sharing of feelings that perhaps came across as being too much for many. Either way, for those who appreciated the emotion that Davis' brought to the table as a frontman, it was clear that he was unafraid to confront painful subjects; he unapologetically put them across with power and strength.

With Davis in the line-up, it wasn't long before Creep changed their name to Korn. Comparatively, Davis was quoted of his time in Sexart in *Kerrang!* in May 2018; "I liked jamming with them, but those guys would tell me what to sing, and would write the lyrics — well, the drummer (Dennis Shinn) did. I was insecure with my singing to begin with, so he took advantage of that. Once I got into Korn, I had no one doing that shit, so I got to do what I wanted to do. I opened up and became a vocalist — I wasn't trying to do what these other fools wanted to do. That was other people in the band — I'm not talking about Ryan (Shuck, Sexart guitarist) or (Dave) DeRoo (bassist)."

With regards to when he joined Korn, Davis was quoted in the same feature; "Seriously, the minute I sang the first song with them, we all looked around at each other and they said, 'You're in the band.' When I heard the demos with Ross (Robinson), I knew in my heart of hearts that we had something different. When we'd play shows we'd go out there and hit the first chord and everyone's jaw would drop — they'd never heard anything like that before. Now everyone tunes to fucking A."

****

Why Follow The Leader?

Davis' lyrics were such that Korn soon adopted a sound that was eerie and sinister. Ironically perhaps, it sounded fresh and innovative. The band soon rented a studio at Underground Chicken Sound and recorded a demo called *Neidermayer's Mind*. Consisting of four songs, it included substantially different versions of 'Daddy' and 'Blind' which Davis had brought over from Sexart. Both songs would eventually be re-interpreted for Korn's self-titled debut album, defining the nu-metal era. Not necessarily as Korn saw it, but still.

Silveria was quoted in *Rolling Stone* in December 2014; "Honestly, when we were labelled the band that invented the style of, what do they call it, "nu rock?" I guess people say we invented this nu-metal sound or whatever. I never really thought of it like that. I just thought we were doing our thing. That's just what came naturally from all our influences as musicians. I never really thought, 'Hey, we've invented this new kind of music, this is going to be huge.' Thought never even crossed my mind."

To make the demo, Korn used the services of one unknown twenty-six-year-old producer, Ross Robinson. Regarding his first impressions of Jonathon Davis, Robinson was quoted in *Rolling Stone* in December 2014; "Basically, he was a goth kid with this kind of funky, dry hair, wearing Monkey Boots, and he was wearing Robert Smith makeup. The band wasn't dark yet; it had killer grooves and good riffs, but there was some happy edge to it. And when he walked into the room, it went dark and goth. Basically, during the first song, to audition in the rehearsal room, he started freaking the hell out. You couldn't hear his voice, but you felt chills all over your body, and it was instantly like, 'Oh my God, yeah — he's the one'."

Davis was quoted in *The Independent* in May 2017; "When I got into the band Ross was all giddy. He came and listened to me sing and said, 'We gotta get in there and do a demo now!' I'd only been in the band for two weeks when we recorded *Neidermayer's Mind* and the songs were done really quickly; they had to be because we were ripping off time from W.A.S.P. They were in the studio doing one of their records and they'd leave around midnight, so Ross would sneak us in and we'd use the studio at night until they came back in the morning. The opening riff to 'Blind' on that demo was played on one of Blackie Lawless's guitars without him even fucking knowing about it."

Davis was quoted in *Rolling Stone* in December 2014; "Fucking crazy-ass Ross. I remember sleeping in a garage with him when he was living in a garage. I had to fucking quit my job where I was making great money as a mortician, had my own house, to fucking having nothing, working at a pizza place as a shift manager living under some stairs."

****

Neidermayer's Mind was poorly received. Still though, with determination and by deciding to tour, it was a performance at California's Huntington Beach that resulted in Korn being signed to Immortal/Epic records. Whilst getting signed was a fantastic opportunity that was a vital step in Korn's journey to becoming a household name, in 1993, the label wasn't quite sure where to place them. They were just so different. As a result, they ended up being the support act for others across a diversity of musical styles; No Doubt, The Offspring, House Of Pain, Marilyn Manson and Pennywise.

Davis was quoted in *New Musical Express* in September 2019; "Oh man, that scene was full of misogynistic, opportunistic dickhead jocks. The sort of people who'd be bullying me at school if they weren't supporting my band at shows. I'm about the art. We got lumped in with that stuff kinda because of the way we dressed. We were kinda hip-hop, but there was nothing really hip-hop about Korn other than the basslines to an extent. I didn't rap! In the beginning nobody knew what we were — we'd play shows with No Doubt or Pennywise and then when the metal community embraced us we went with it because it felt like we'd found a home."

He was quoted in *The Independent* in May 2017; "They just didn't know where to put us. I always felt like we were a black sheep; to me, metal bands are Judas Priest and Iron Maiden, shit like that. We were nothing like them; we were more of a funk band if anything, more about grooves and heaviness. When the nu-metal tag came out, I was like 'whatever, you've got to call it something' but I like the fact that we were such outcasts. It was very surreal back then but we knew we were doing something cool and different just from the reaction we were getting."

He was quoted in *The Guardian* in October 2016; "We totally destroyed what people thought the metal scene should be. I always felt weird in metal culture. I was always fighting the title of what a metal band was."

In response to the interviewer's comment of "What's interesting about Korn's music is how some people have said Korn is "heavy metal", but you have said that some people say that you're trying to kill "heavy metal".", Davis said in a press release for *Follow The Leader*; "Yeah. Heavy metal to me is like Iron Maiden, Helloween, those heavy metal bands. Not the glam bands. But they've always called us heavy metal and it fuckin' pisses me off because that's just fucked up. They put us in that category, but I don't know what to call it. No one has come up with a really good fuckin' name to call this. Nirvana had grunge and I guess that was cool. But there's been emo-core, heavy-hop, post-metal and nu-metal. None of those really ring a bell."

Head was quoted of Korn's first album in *Rolling Stone* in December 2014; "We were into everything, from Pantera to Ice Cube. We liked the samples on the Cypress Hill stuff. The first record was about mimicking some of the hip-hop stuff that was going on in that day."

When it came to making their first album, the studio environment was a familiar one. Davis was quoted in *Rolling Stone* in December 2014; "Walking in there and seeing all the crazy, old-school analogue gear. I knew what this shit was because my dad had a recording studio. The shit that was in that studio, my dad dreamed about, and I just saw in pictures. I'm sitting there looking at it, going, 'Oh my God, that's an API Console!'."

The character of the studio perhaps informed the musical innovation on the album. Robinson was quoted in the same feature; "Richard (Kaplan, Indigo Ranch Studio owner) had a big ol' box of seventies guitar pedals. That first Korn album was the first metal album to really use guitar pedals. I'm such a fan of that feeling you get when you hear Manfred Mann's Earth Band's 'Blinded By The Light', when that phaser kicks in — Indigo had that exact phaser. I really believe that is the first metal album to start the pedal trend, for sure. We didn't walk in there like that; it was ready and waiting for us... I didn't know what the hell I was doing at all. When I didn't know the answer to something, I would go to the bathroom and put my head on the floor and ask for help until I got this chill in my body. Then I would go out and have all the answers to know what to do."

Everyone had a vision for the sound that they wanted to create. Fieldy was quoted in *Rolling Stone* in December 2014; "I had to battle with Ross because I knew the sound I wanted — that real percussion-y, click-y sound. He would mic up my cabinet and I'd go in there and I'd play. I'm like, 'That's not my tone, that's not my tone.' He'd move it in another part of the speaker, I go, 'That's not my tone.' Finally he just grabbed the mic and put it right in the centre, right on the horn. I go, 'That's my tone.' He just got tired of my mouth." Davis was quoted in the same feature; "I remember when we started up 'Clown', David (Silveria) was refusing to start the song, 'cause he didn't understand what was going on and I was getting frustrated and talking shit to him. It was irritating." Silveria: "One guy was telling me four clicks, and another guy was telling me no clicks. And I was saying, 'How are we supposed to start the song if there's no clicks?'."

Davis recalled, "Ross loved just keeping the tape recorder going and capturing that shit. Everybody credits Ross as making our sound, but it was us. The root of the whole thing was us. He fine-tuned shit though, and I'm not gonna deny he helped... The whole thing was, in the studio, the tones and everything were our ideas."

Korn's image was as unusual as their music. Davis was quoted in *Metal Hammer* in January 2019; "I loved our tracksuits! I grew up listening to old industrial music and dark gothic music, but at the time I was a big hip-hop fan, and I liked it because it was just so off — it was so not what this music is. That's what I'm all about, like, 'What the fuck is going on? Why is this guy wearing a tracksuit and coming out playing bagpipes?'"

The unusual image worked though; fans didn't hesitate to emulate it. Fieldy was quoted in *Exposure* in December 1996; "They show up with Brian's hair, David's goatee, all five of us in one person, it's trippy." Fieldy was quoted in *Rolling Stone* in December 2014; "I started seeing everybody showing up wearing Adidas." It was advocated in *Billboard* in December 2000; "By introducing its Adidas-covered, funk-metal hybrid to a post-grunge world, Korn set both the fashion and form for today's hard music scene."

****

Korn's 1994 debut album is considered by many to have pioneered the genre that came to be known as nu-metal. It was the album that introduced Korn to a generation of fans. The thought that went into making the album certainly paid off. Robinson was quoted in *Rolling Stone* in December 2014; "We spent $14,000 on that first album — that was our budget. The reason I picked (Indigo Ranch Studio) was because Neil Young was there, Neil Diamond, all these really killer old-schoolers. I think Lenny Kravitz recorded there, Nick Cave. I knew that recording raw and vintage, the album wouldn't sound dated ever. So we didn't have any of the eighties reverbs."

Whilst Korn's debut album only charted as high as number seventy-two on the Billboard 200 chart and reviews were dramatically varied, the album opened the door for what was to follow. Davis was quoted in *Rolling Stone* in December 2014; "(The album) sold eleven hundred copies in the first week. I was fucking so excited. And then shit started going more and more. When we went out on Ozzy's tour, Ozzy walked in with a bottle of champagne with Sharon and a gold record and presented us our gold record. I'll never fucking forget that 'cause Ozzy's my fucking hero."

To which Silveria was quoted; "I guess our managers had sent the gold records out on the road for them to surprise us with. And when we saw that we had sold half a million records, that was the first time I really felt, 'Wow, this was really going to take off'."

With lyrics full of angst that spoke strongly of alienation, something about Korn got through to young listeners in a different way to what previous heavy metal music had done. Davis was quoted of his choice in subject matters on *Korn* in *Vice* in September 2019; "On the first record, I was just getting the shit out, I didn't know it was gonna spark or so many people were going to be taken back by or feel some kind of relief by it."

Fans welcomed Korn's unique sound. Tracks such as 'Daddy' and 'Faget' touched on the taboo topics of abuse and yet, the lyrics had universal appeal in terms of how they referenced feelings of helplessness and alienation. Davis was quoted in *The Guardian* in October 2016; "We were little kids when we made our first record. I had no idea then that my pain would help so many people."

He was quoted in *Melody Maker* in May 1999: "I went through a new romantic phase and I had the make-up, the frilly shirt, all that shit. I stuck out, I was this big dork, basically, and I suffered for it greatly. I was picked on, called a faggot. Just because I wore makeup and they didn't know how to deal with it. I got my ass kicked a couple of times. I was shoved and kicked and the teachers would laugh and call me a faggot. They even sent me to a gay counsellor. Everyone was telling me I'm gay, I'm gay and I didn't know if I was. So I tried to be with a guy and it was totally disgusting, but I had to find out. Because everyone in the fucking world was telling me I was. Even my own father was embarrassed of me. I'd come to work at his music store and he'd go, 'That's some kid I hired'."

The language of Davis' lyrics brought something very new to listeners' ears. Whilst it wasn't unheard of for songs to address taboo subjects prior to Korn, they were often communicated through metaphors that could easily be interpreted differently to suit the whims of the listener (and indeed, the image that a band may have preferred to portray). In Davis' lyrics, he was explicitly literal in how he referenced issues such as abuse, addiction and depression.

Further to this though, it was Davis' delivery of the lyrics that gave them the edge that became so associated with Korn's sound. In particular, on the track, 'Daddy', Davis broke down hysterically in the recording studio, thus lending Korn's music to an extent of voyeurism.

Robinson was quoted in *Rolling Stone* in December 2014; "(On 'Daddy') I remember just telling Jon, 'You know what to do.' That's all I said."

Davis: "It was just a special moment that I didn't know was being recorded, for one, because Ross is a prick and kept the fuckin' tape running."

Robinson: "And it's all live. No overdubs."

Head was quoted on the recording process of 'Daddy' in *Rolling Stone* in December 2014; "It was one of the most intense things I ever witnessed in my life. It was so crazy; I thought he was joking at first 'cause he was really bawling and everything. But it was very, very intense."

To which Silveria was quoted; "When we ended the song, Jonathan was still crying. I could see him through the window, from the drum booth. He was actually on the floor crying and Ross was in the control room, talking in our in-ears, going, 'Keep going!' making a rolling motion with his hand. So we just kept going."

Davis: "And I remember that moment, when I came out of there, and I was fucking sobbing, my whole band was crying, and they just all hugged me and shit. It was a crazy fucking experience. It was the good ol' days, dude. We were all a band of brothers. We were like the fucking Three Musketeers — everybody was there for all their parts."

Fieldy: "I remember crying on that song. I was just crying on of how heavy and powerful the song was, and it just made me emotional."

The emotional honesty in Korn's music, particularly on their first album, has often been attributed to Ross Robinson's production. Drawing intense and painful emotion out of vocalists is something that Robinson became known for as his career developed. It eventually became too much for Korn when it came to making *Follow The Leader* but still, it was certainly an iconic ingredient when it came to making the debut album.

Davis was quoted in *The Independent* in May 2017; "I think we both helped each other figure out what our roles were on that first record. Breaking down in 'Daddy' and all that other emotionally open shit, that was all coming from me. That stuff just happened and Ross was smart enough to keep the tape rolling. We grew together, I have nothing but love for Ross, I just feel sorry for the bands he works with."

Davis was quoted of Robinson in *Rolling Stone* in December 2014; "He's a fucking sadistic bastard, that motherfucker. I love him, though; don't get me wrong. But yeah, I think it gets him off. When I was twenty-three, I didn't know any better. I thought all producers were like this until after, when we did all the rest of our records where they started becoming fun. He had his way and was digging in to me and pulling shit out. I was already writing stuff about it, but to get the performance out, he really just poured salt on the wound."

To which Robinson said; "It was simply one hundred percent belief in everything he was saying and one hundred percent loyalty to being in an extremely comfortable place for him, where he felt so safe with me that nothing bad would ever happen. I was doing a lot of my mum's (self-help author Byron Katie) early workshops — she was starting back then, but now she's world-famous — but those early workshops with her, it was normal to see people reveal the deepest, deepest, darkest secrets that no one's supposed to know."

Head: "I think Jonathan doesn't give himself a lot of credit. A lot of us have things that come to the surface that we maybe have to deal with later in life — childhood things come up. Jonathan was going through that then, so he was singing about it, and it was like therapy to him. So it was coming out of him anyway. Ross would try to bring it out of him. But it was a team effort, definitely. Back then, he didn't beat Jonathan up. He pulled it out of him."

It was on that debut album that the bagpipes became established as part of the band's distinctive sound. Davis' great-grandmother was from Scotland and often listened to traditional music. This, combined with the fact that he was roused by Mr Scott playing 'Amazing Grace' on the bagpipes at the funeral of Mr Spock in the 1982 film, *Star Trek II: The Wrath Of Khan*, inspired Davis to begin playing the instrument from a young age.

When Korn were recording the track, 'Shoots And Ladders', it was felt that there was something missing from what was already a good song. It was at this point that Davis' bagpipe skills were welcomed to the band and they proved to be a vital part of Korn's sound from that moment on. Davis said of the bagpipes in *New Musical Express* in September 2019; "The greatest instrument in the fucking world!"

In the USA alone, *Korn* went on to sell over two million. It started the ball rolling for Korn and indeed a number of bands who would go on to try and emulate their sound. Just two and a half years after its release, the album went platinum. It was perfect timing as *Life Is Peachy* was just beginning to give Korn more of a profile on MTV. Davis was quoted in *Vice* in September 2019; "I was twenty fucking four — who the fuck knew? I didn't know it was going to be such a big thing,"

****

As many successful bands experience, a high-impact debut album can put the pressure on when it comes to doing the second album. In this regard, Korn were no exception. As a result, whilst *Life Is Peachy* did well enough commercially and contains tracks that have gone on to be iconic staples in Korn's live sets, although at the time, Korn felt that their second album was a rushed job.

Head said in 2018 "It had its moments, but half of us didn't really like *Life Is Peachy* compared to the first album."

Fieldy told *Kerrang!* in January 1999; "I guess everything we do is kind of sarcastic. *Life Is Peachy* had nothing to do with life being peachy or not. A peachy is a kind of folder at high school."

In *Billboard* in July 1998, Davis was reported to have said; "I just wasn't happy with the way the last one (*Life Is Peachy*) came out. We settled on the last one to get it out quickly."

However, not long after the release of *Life Is Peachy*, there were instances where Korn felt that it still moved them forward from their first album. In *Exposure* in December 1996 Davis said of the lyrics in *Life Is Peachy*; "I've matured more. I'm not crying about my childhood anymore. The first record was just, get that shit out."

It was considered in *Billboard* in May 2002; "*Life Is Peachy* offered a more musically mature Korn, with improved song structures and slightly more pop tones creeping into still-heavy compositions like 'Twist' and 'Good God'."

Life Is Peachy was not without the emotional rawness that Korn had become known for with the first album. Davis was quoted in *Rolling Stone* in December 2014; "Honestly, I don't think it was that bad on the first record. I think I was just letting shit go and he was just going with it. He (Robinson) didn't start to get into that shit until the second Korn record. I remember him starting to bring up my stepmom, which I hated, and all kinds of shit like that. Shit that he knew pushed my buttons and got me going... He figured out his production style on us. And then he just went and took it to the next level with other bands. But I don't think he quite fucked people up like he did me. I think I'm his favourite."

Whether or not Korn were pleased with *Life Is Peachy*, by summer 1997, things were on the up as the band headlined on the Lollapalooza tour alongside acts such as Tool and Snoop Dog. It increased their profile overall. However, Korn only played fourteen out of the twenty seven dates for Lollapalooza due to Munky taking ill. Silveria asserted in a press release; "It was kind of a disappointment, because all of us in the band had wanted to play Lollapalooza for so long. We were excited about doing it. After Munky had been in the hospital for a few days rather than a couple of days — like when it turned into five or six days — everyone started getting really worried about him. Then we said we should probably take him out of the hospital, take him home to LA, get him treatment there and get him better, because no tour was worth anyone's personal health. We were not going to drag it on and have him sitting in a hospital feeling this weight on him thinking everyone was counting the hours for him to get up and come back to the tour and play. It was disappointing at first about the tour, but everyone was cool with it because we knew it was Munky's personal health that was at stake here. That is more important than a tour. The business aspect of it was just something we had to deal with."

With regards to this situation, Davis said in a press release for *Follow The Leader*; "I was pissed, but I was more worried about Munky anyway. But when I found out we had to pull off I wasn't pissed at him, I was just pissed that he got sick because we were just having fun. We could have played without him, but we chose to pull off, because we weren't going to play without him. It was hard, but we were worried for Munky. We wanted him to be fine and we wanted him to get home and get well so we could start working on the next album."

Endearingly, Korn were united in a brotherly way; there is a strong sense that they really cared about each other as people. Whilst another musician could have been hired, Korn continuously maintained that they wouldn't have been happy to go down that route.

Davis was quoted in *Kerrang!* in 1998; "When Munky got sick halfway through the Lollapalooza tour, we could easily have got someone in to replace him but that would be ripping our fans off. It's not Korn with one of us missing. Munky is okay now. He's been taking care of himself. He's been on a sobriety trip for about three or four months. If he drinks again, he'll get his game face back on: When you go back on tour, you're drinking and you're back in character, I guess. You get your "game face" back. But the Lollapalooza thing fucking tore Munky up. He didn't say anything, but I know it did. I know how it feels. Fuck, I've cancelled shows on the band, pissing off fans and losing us tons of money. I've felt like shit, but shit happens. We couldn't be mad at the guy — we just wanted him to fucking live! I wanted to stay on the tour but fuck, I want Munky around!"

It was still a tentative time because with two successful albums behind them and with many new bands trying to ape their sound, for Korn, it was a question of "what next?" As part of this, challenges with addiction and mental health were coming to the fore. Davis was quoted in *Melody Maker* in May 1999: "I'd get panic attacks when I woke up and have them all day. I don't like medical drugs because I don't like being doped up, so I'd be going through all kinds of hell. I got schizophrenic and psychotic and I stopped eating because I thought people were poisoning my food, and these were all the side affects of panic... They'd come on for no reason. So it's horrible. And the only time I felt good was when I was onstage. And then a couple of times I had the attacks onstage. I'd freak out because everyone was staring at me."

Korn - *Follow The Leader*: In-depth

With 1994's *Korn* and 1996's *Life Is Peachy* behind them, Korn's early success was reasonable but there was still a mountain to be climbed in view of the fact that the band had faced a lot of hostility from music critics and had built their fanbase from touring. Certainly, it wasn't from radio play.

That fanbase was looking forward to a third album. Steve Barnett, senior VP of worldwide marketing at Epic, was quoted in *Billboard* in July 1998; "The anticipation for this record is very much on a global basis. Korn have sold four million albums worldwide and the impressive thing about it is that they've done that under the radar. We've been able to achieve this with zero radio play. The touring base has played a major part in their success internationally."

Epic's rock promoter, Ron Cerrito, was quoted in *Radio & Records* in November 1999; "Korn played three hundred dates the first year — with no radio airplay! We initially shipped it to metal and college radio. It was more about exposure and creating a buzz than about rotations and creating a hit song. When we did go to commercial radio, we had some limited success in certain markets where people were willing to step out. Every time that happened, we saw an increase in sales. But the band was built on constant touring. With the second album we saw radio come on board a little more, and that helped sales big time. The third album provided big airplay and big sales... With artists like Korn, we look at artist development in terms of getting an audience interested in a band, then going to radio and showing them their audience is buying the album and buying tickets to see the concert. That's what helps us get a Korn record, which is different, on the air... Radio can help us take the artist to a whole new level."

Really, it was the success of *Follow The Leader* that finally made Korn's music credible for radio play. Silveria told *Spin* in November 1998; "I can't believe we're finally a radio band."

Davis was quoted in *Radio & Records* in August 1998; "The coolest thing about this band is we've stayed underground and our fans are still so true. They're so militant and crazy about us." *Follow The Leader* changed the scale of Korn's operation. It was reported in the same feature; "Keep an ear out for 'Got The Life' which is screaming quite loudly across the air nationwide."

Overall, Korn's first album had been a slow burner; it was successful but it took some time to gain momentum, teamed with the arrival of *Life Is Peachy* in 1996. As the band's third album, *Follow The Leader* was the turning point in terms of being able to fully utilise the power of MTV and youth marketing on a larger scale. With vast promotion came an inflated image in the public eye in the days before the Internet had really taken off.

Commercially, Korn were sponsored generously. Davis told *The Independent* in May 2017; "We're one of the last of a string of bands that sold out arenas, that had big budget videos, that lived fucking larger than life; it was crazy, we lost all sense of who we were for a while there. I had to walk around with two bodyguards twenty hours a fucking day. We used to play gigs, hang out in the crowd, pass out tapes, go to keg parties and all that shit but after that album blew up, all of that was gone. It was an insane time, all of us were going a little cuckoo and got a bit cocky but that's because you lose your life. To this day, I still can't go nowhere in the world without being recognised. I don't expect people to understand that unless you go through it but it's fucking nuts! We were partying every night and I was at the height of my insanity. I got sober in '98 because it all became too much, I either had to kick that shit or die."

Korn had a strong reputation for how they liked to party. It was certainly no secret. Davis was quoted of his 27th birthday party in *Kerrang!* in March 1998; "My party was the shit. Everybody and their Ma was there. Fabrice from Milli Vanilli was there! There was some bondage chick getting beat, and strippers. They brought in this big vagina cake and shoved my face in the middle of it. Then, all of a sudden, a guy came in playing the bagpipes with Barney from *The Flintstones* marching behind him! Fucking insane!"

Even before the party days of recording *Follow The Leader*, it comes across that Davis was considering the importance of slowing down. "I've been chilling out. I still get fucked up, but I've gotta chill, he said in March 1998. "I've got to do it for my kid and for everybody else in the band. Fucking seriously. All those times I said I was gonna die, this time I really am. I can feel it. I've had heart palpitations and shit. I've been having hangovers so bad I couldn't get out of bed for three days. That's not fun."

Davis reached such an extent of fame that it became necessary for him to have a bodyguard and this is still the case to this very day. He was quoted in *The Ringer* in August 2018; "It was Britney Spears, Backstreet Boys, and fuckin' NSYNC at the time. We were the only rock band on *Total Request Live* that was doing that shit. I had people showing up to my house trying to jump the fences to get in, all kinds of crazy shit."

'Freak On A Leash' was popular on MTV at a time where bubblegum pop was prominent in the mainstream. Korn stood out. It could be said that their music was part of an important movement that brought a new form of hard rock, nu-metal, to the fore. Korn's rise to success in the late nineties was part of an interesting diversification of music. It started to become a norm that rock would embrace hip-hop and rap would include heavy metal elements. Limp Bizkit, Linkin Park, Papa Roach and even Eminem all took part in such use of fusion to an extent. Munky was quoted in *The Fader* in August 2018; "I felt it was good for our up-and-coming genre that was about to break. It gave kids a place in this pop-driven world —an alternative option for that generation."

Of course though, inspiration has to come from somewhere and Korn's came from a variety of interesting artists. Davis told *The Fader* in August 2018; "*Korn* and *Life Is Peachy* were similar. With *Follow The Leader*, we started to experiment with more hip-hop-inspired basslines mixed with rock guitar, making the guitar sound like samples. I've said it a billion times, but if it wasn't for Cypress Hill there would be no Korn."

Talking about his pre-Korn performing style the same month in *The Ringer* he said; "I was a mixture of Jim Morrison, fucking Robert Smith, and Rakim."

Upon being asked which albums most inspired his imagination, Davis said, "There were two: Peter Gabriel's *Passion* (the 1989 soundtrack for Martin Scorsese's film *The Last Temptation Of Christ*) and *The Serpent's Egg* by (Australian band) Dead Can Dance (in 1988). They were both cool, worldly records that took me to a different place. You could put them on, immerse yourself, and forget about your life."

Davis said in a *Follow The Leader* press release; "The only thing that influences me is the eighties. I love that era. It was all just so musical. Everything was just fucking exciting. In every aspect of all the music: the goth scene, the industrial scene, the fuckin' new wave scene and the metal scene, everything was so new and fuckin' awesome. And it just seems that the nineties have totally just sucked, especially the alternative thing. The only thing that was good was the grunge movement. We killed everything. But stuff like Duran Duran, Culture Club — those melodies were incredible. They were all great. I mean, look how many hits Devo had! Like 'Whip It'. All those songs. Just one after another. All that shit was really good and fun to listen to. It wasn't like this cheesy alternative shit right now. So yeah, I'd say that the eighties stuff — that way of singing — truly influenced me. I dug all that shit."

Taking perhaps a more of a holistic approach with regards to influences, Silveria asserted; "There's music that I like to listen to, but when it comes to writing our music, I don't really get influenced by anyone else's music. I get influenced as we write our music. The part comes up and it influences me to think a certain way about the part and about how to go about writing to it... What we are contributing is high-energy music, intense, aggressive music, fun music. And I think there are more mellow-style bands doing the softer alternative, poppy kind of sound. I think the scene needed a little bit more of the intense, high-energy music, which we're bringing to the fans."

When *Follow The Leader* was released in 1998, the impact of the album took Korn to dizzying new heights beyond the existing cult following. The album put Korn on the map, as well as their innovative brand of music.

Chapter Two
The Making of Follow The Leader

Munky said to *Metal Hammer* in December 2018; "It kinda felt we'd coined this sound and then we were trying to follow it up with something we'd already done. So when *Follow The Leader* came around it was either we're gonna make the same record for the next twenty five years or we're gonna be a band that evolves. I think that was the turning point."

Each member brought their own musical interests to the table, a vital ingredient in the making of *Follow The Leader*. Fieldy told *The Fader*; "Everyone was into different things. I was into newer-school hip-hop, the guitar players were into rock music."

Regarding the hybrid of musical influences present on *Follow The Leader*, Davis stated in a press release for the album; "We just stick to that sick, weird, eerie vibe and then throw hip-hop elements into it. It's strange, I don't know how to explain it. We just do what we do to be honest. It's also a combination of all our different influences — there's no big heads in our band. Everybody's got their little bits that they put in. Like Fieldy with his hip-hop influences. Me with my melodies and all my eighties drama that I love. Munky is always into John Zorn and the Mr Bungle stuff and so is Head. So I think it just creates a cool musical cocktail or whatever you want to call it. Yeah, it's putting chaos into music. Because all the sounds are all dissonant and just fucked up. It's not really all in key. It all melts together into something that's got melody."

It was in a small studio in Redondo Beach that Korn began writing songs for their third album. Davis said; "We were writing by ourselves in a little studio — just a room with a PA. It was nothing special, just us with the music."

Munky was quoted of *Follow The Leader* in *Total Guitar* in September 1998; "All the songs are new. We had to get off the tour and take some time off before we could go back to the creative process. We can't write on the road because we'd turn into some sort of Bob Seger figure, and today's kids would like that — we wouldn't like it!"

Head told *The Fader*; "We were in a good headspace. We were all like one — no issues with band members or anything. We were still climbing up and doing theatres, touring with bands like Deftones and opening for bigger bands like Megadeth, Ozzy and all them. We were in the studio without any producer or leader, just us friends hanging out. That would come to an end after that record."

Having penned a few songs, Korn made their way to a different studio. Unlike their first two albums however, it wasn't with Ross Robinson and it wasn't at Indigo Ranch. Munky said to *Kerrang!* in July 1998; "With this record, we wanted to get a new producer and take a whole new approach. We're still Korn."

NRG Studio B was quite the upgrade technically. It had plenty of space and was equipped with several rooms. This gave Korn the perfect opportunity for working on loops and for practicing individual parts of songs before recording them. The studio also lent itself to an intense party environment due to the number of people who were constantly passing through.

Having shown their commercial potential already, when it came to making *Follow The Leader*, Epic liberally handed Korn an artistic blank cheque. It resulted in them having the time to interview for a new producer. Whilst Robinson had been a key part of their first two albums, it was felt that it was time to change the sound as well as the methods used in generating the more emotional elements of making an album.

It perhaps wasn't the worst move for Robinson either, given his experiences during the first two albums. He told *Loudwire* in August 2019; "There were girls in the studio all the time when they were supposedly working, and they had people involved with them who were giving them blow. I wasn't involved with the drug scene or the party scene with those guys. I was the straight edge dude and the one they trusted the most. But basically their vision got clouded. They hired people to party with. As soon as that whole scene turned completely into Mötley Crüe I was out of the picture."

Korn opted for Steve Thompson as a producer on something of a whim. Davis was quoted in *Kerrang!* in March 1998; "Steve is a really good guy. I like him and it's cool that he's doing our album... We had so many meetings with people but couldn't find anybody who was on our level and had a clue. We could tell, just by having lunch with 'em. One guy didn't even know we went platinum! He was just doing it for the fucking cheque. Some other guys did ska bands, Queensrÿche, Alice Cooper and shit. That wasn't for us. From ska to Korn. I don't know! Steve was the last guy. He came in all fucking 'Noo Yawk' with a whole bunch of beer, so obviously he watched our home video. He was maybe trying to kiss up our ass too much. It was fucking funny, but we were like 'don't know about this dude', but we thought we'd give him a chance. He came in, working on one song and he worked great with us. He had great ideas and inspired us to do other shit. We thought 'fuck it! Let's do it.'... Arrangement wise, when you write songs, you need an outside ear to hear how the song flows. It's nit-picking. Chopping shit here and there, to make it fucking interesting. He made the song better than it was in the first place. If he hadn't worked out, we were gonna get Ross back... It was just a matter of saying 'Ross, we've done two albums with you. They were great albums, but it's time for us to move on.' If you do the same thing enough times, kids are gonna get bored and so will the band. We're trying for a different sound this time, and Ross is totally cool with it. He's upset, I know. It's his baby, his love. But parents have gotta let their kids go sometime!"

Choosing to go with a new producer was a bold move considering that Ross Robinson had made a significant contribution to the overall feel of both *Korn* and *Life Is Peachy*. Head was quoted in *Metal Hammer* in December 2018; "We just wanted to try something new. Ross was an awesome, ground-breaking producer who taught us a lot, but he was a leader, and the best leaders should be able to train people and then send them out. And I feel that's just what Ross did...

and then we wanted to go and do our own thing. Ross had really trained us well with melodies and doing weird sounds with the guitar, so we took it another step. The band wrote all the music together and a couple of producers worked on the record. It's been said in a blog that our songs were a mess when we sent them in, but they were not a mess — they were just like they are. There were a couple of tweaks, but the structures were all in place for almost the entire record."

Davis was missing working with Robinson — to an extent — but things soon reached breaking point again when he was invited back into the studio. Davis was quoted in *The Fader* in August 2018; "It was my first record without Ross Robinson, so I had Ross come in and produce the vocals with me. He was doing some crazy weird shit like sticking his nails in my back when I was singing… He was doing this weird method acting shit and I was just like, 'I did that and it was cool, but I'm past this shit with you, Ross. No offense, I love you brother, but I'm trying to do something different. I don't need to have you put your fucking nails in my back and make me hurt to feel the pain.' So he peeled back a little bit… He was my crutch. I was very afraid to do an album without him — that's all I'd known. He came in for a couple songs and then I didn't need him anymore and he was like, 'Cool, it's all good, no hard feelings.' I did the rest with Toby."

To which Toby Wright was quoted; "Jonathan did hire him very briefly as his vocal coach. One of the first things Ross did while Jonathan was trying to sing was punch him in the back, right on his spine. A couple of times. I was like, 'That can't happen. Why are you punching the singer while he's singing? I don't understand this method.'… He's a very violent person. I've heard stories of him throwing chairs, guitars, all kinds of stuff at people while they're playing. I don't think it lasted more than two or three vocal sessions."

Upon being asked "How did Robinson feel when you told him you wanted him back?", Davis was quoted in *Kerrang!* in July 1998; "He was fucking stoked! But he wasn't involved in the whole production thing — he was just like a glorified cheerleader."

Davis was quoted in *The Ringer* in August 2018; "No disrespect to Ross (Robinson), because I love him dearly, but he was a sadist."

Robinson told *Spin* in November 1998; "I've always been into working with the kid who was beaten up and kicked around because the most creative stuff will come out of them. And that's Korn."

Despite what Steve Thompson was considered to have brought to the album initially, Korn called in Toby Wright to finish off the production. Wright had previously worked with Alice In Chains, Metallica and Slayer. Wright's experience was such that it opened the door to further experimentation. On the experimentation front, Korn were particularly effective when it came to collaborating with other artists; Ice Cube, Tre Hardson of The Pharcyde, Fred Durst and Cheech. In some cases, the guest list that features on *Follow The Leader* was pretty spontaneous.

In a press release for the album, Davis said of the track, 'All In The Family'; "That song was originally for B-Real (of Cypress Hill) and it didn't work out 'cause his record label wouldn't let him do it. Fred (Durst of Limp Bizkit) was at the studio one day after a Korn TV taping, and we said, 'Let's do a song together. Hey, man, let's go back and forth and rip on each other like an old-school battle.' I don't know whose idea it was. I can't remember if it was mine, or Fieldy's, or Fred's, but we came up with the idea and we started writing and we worked on it together. I even came up with some bags on myself for Fred to say. It was all in good natured fun."

Davis said in *The Boston Globe* in August 1998; "It's just me and him ragging on each other. Some kids think that Korn and Limp Bizkit hate each other. But hey, why we would be in the same room talking to each other if we hated each other? We have total respect."

A cover of Cheech & Chong's 'Earache My Eye' was included as a bonus track. Davis said in *Loudwire* in August 2019; "That was done just for fun and we laughed our asses off making it. Of course we were high as fuck, but I think it's really important to do shit like that from time to time just to keep things in perspective. If you're a musician and you're serious all the time you're fucked."

'My Gift To You' stops at 7:12 into the track and is followed by two minutes of silence. At 9:12, 'Earache My Eye' starts playing after an anecdote from Fieldy recorded during the studio session. As dark as some of the themes are on *Follow The Leader*, it wasn't all doom and gloom.

Munky told *Metal Hammer* in December 2018; "I think the Cheech thing came about from Fieldy. He loves smoking weed! It's the funniest thing, because he used to hate it, and then he went through this weed phase, watching all the Cheech & Chong movies. Then we were messing around in the studio playing (*Life Is Peachy*'s War cover) 'Lowrider', and he was like, 'Wouldn't it be awesome if we could get Cheech in the studio!' He was a super-nice guy and he brought his family to the show, later in that tour cycle. Then Ice Cube came into the studio and that was the first time I'd witnessed a real pro, someone that came in and killed it. He listened to the track a few times, studied it, didn't talk much and was very serious about his craft. I was blown away and it was really inspiring."

Starstruck at meeting Ice Cube, Head said to *Metal Hammer* in December 2018; "My heart was pounding! I had to come up with a cool riff and not let him down, and I'm shaking! Pressure! It was surreal, dude. When I was nineteen or twenty I was all over N.W.A. The realness and the rawness — and Ice Cube's voice tones were just the best."

On meeting Ice Cube, Fieldy said in *Kerrang!* in January 1999; "We actually first met him when we did a cover of The Clash song, 'Should I Stay Or Should I Go?' for Mack 10's *The Recipe* record. We didn't know what to expect, but when we got there he came across like a professional with no attitude whatsoever. Totally cool and excited about music." Munky was quoted in *Guitarist* in October 1998; "The reason we did stuff with Ice Cube is because he approached us! We're all really big fans of his and all the acts on the N.W.A. label so that was cool, he was great to work with. It was good to do something in the Run-DMC and Aerosmith tradition — 'Walk This Way' just has to be the best song."

In a press release for *Follow The Leader*, Davis said of 'Children Of The Korn'; "Cube came up with the title. I fed off of what he wrote — he was talking about growing up during puberty, and having people dictate to him what he can do, like 'how you gonna tell me how to live and who to fuck.' And in one of my verses, I'm talking about being a kid that's always known as the fuckin' town faggot. It's funny how things change — how some of these people picked on me and all of a sudden, look who's laughing now, because I'm a big rock star now. And in another verse, I talk about all these parents fuckin' hating me for what I do, saying I'm corrupting their children, but in turn these parents need to step outside of themselves and really listen to what I'm talking about. Then I think they can understand that they were kids before. They're just really quick to judge me. All the 'Children Of The Korn' are all our Korn fans. All those kids going thought that shit and feeling what I feel."

'Freak On A Leash' starts off as quite a subtle song but it soon evolves into an aggressive drum beat with an intense bridge leading into the chorus. Structurally it's not too different to a pop song. Clearly though, the mood of the song — and the mood alone — makes it clear that 'Freak On A Leash' and indeed Korn are definitely not pop music. 'Freak On A Leash' lashes out at life in general as well as making an angry and frustrated dig at the music industry.

Of course, one of the most iconic parts of the song is from the moment Davis shouts "Go!" Whilst 'Got The Life' and 'Freak On A Leash' appealed to a wide audience when released as singles, there are other songs that are more experimental, both in terms of how they blend a number of musical genres and with regards to the exceptionally dark subject matters conveyed.

In a press release for *Follow The Leader*, Davis said of 'It's On!'; "This is my peer pressure song. It's about me, being so stressed out, going out, partying and everybody's just going 'Come on dude, it's on.' That's partying: it's about the alcohol, women and everything else — all that wrapped into one. Like in the chorus when I talk about 'Why am I really doing this?' It's all my fault that I'm doing this because all the booze and the women do is just make it worse. They just rearrange all the problems into a different order so I can deal with them one moment at a time."

'Dead Bodies Everywhere' is characterised by a very low bass part, much guitar distortion and even a music box melody. The lyrical themes are about as dark as it could possibly get. Davis said of the song; "That was about my parents trying to keep me out of the music business. My father was in it and he knew how it was and I totally understand him now that I have a son. I want Nathan to be a musician, but I don't want him to go through the hell I went through. That's the same thing my dad was doing. A lot of people can relate to it, because the dads are wanting their sons to be football players and their sons want to be doctors or something else. That kind of pressure we get from our parents when we're growing up — trying to make their sons into something they're really not. The 'Dead Bodies' thing is how I did just that. I worked at the coroner's office instead of being a musician, and all I got out of it was 'Dead Bodies Everywhere', and I got all traumatised. Thanks a lot mom and dad."

Davis championed 'Pretty' as his favourite song on the album because "it's a bad-ass song. It's just really a beautiful song. It's beautiful chaos... It's a story about this little girl that came into the coroner's office when I was working there and she was fucked by her dad. She was an eleven-month-old little baby girl. Her legs were broken back behind her, and he had raped her like a toy doll and chucked her in the bathroom. It was the most heinous thing I've ever seen in my life and I still have nightmares about it. I was about seventeen and a half at the time. It was heavy man. I went through all kinds of therapy. I found out I have post-traumatic stress disorder from seeing all those bodies, like how American veterans in the Vietnam War got it from seeing all the death around them. When you see someone dead it traumatises your brain. You don't know what to do with all this shit. It's one of the reasons I'm so fucked in the head is because I was so young and my brain couldn't store the stuff. It didn't know what to do with it, so my brain freaks out and causes trauma. That's why I'm afraid of death. I can't talk to people, really. I'm scared to talk to people I don't know. I'm afraid of flying, and I can't drive. I've dealt with the reality of death. Most people think they're not gonna die. Well I never had that chance of denying it 'cause I saw it every fuckin' day. It was the reality of death. It could happen any time, any minute. I live my life everyday like it's gonna be my last. I always gotta go back into the reality in my head that I could die at any minute, and I don't wanna die, because I have so much to live for."

Upon being asked about his time working as an embalmer, Davis was quoted in *Kerrang!* in May 2018; "I got into it because I liked horror movies and all kinds of dark shit. I went on this regional occupation programme where they taught you skills, and of course I wanted to learn how to do autopsies, because I thought it would be fucking cool. But lo and behold, little did I know that that shit would fuck me up for a long time. I saw some really fucked-up shit, which at the time made me a really hard, no-emotions motherfucker. I had post-traumatic stress from seeing dead babies, and young kids that had died after finding a parent's stash of drugs — shit that I shouldn't have been seeing at sixteen or seventeen years old. I had to have a lot of therapy to make the nightmares go away, but I got through it and it made me appreciate life a lot more."

Notably, Davis' response to the subject in more recent years is different to what it perhaps used to be. In May 1999 in *Melody Maker*, he was quoted of his time in mortuary college; "It intrigued me and I loved it. I've pulled so many dead bodies out of cars. It's like a puzzle. Trying to figure out how someone died. It gave me attention too. It was fucking weird. I got into it for attention and ended up liking it."

Upon being asked whether he could relate to Davis' lyrics, Silveria asserted; "Personally, I didn't have a bad childhood, but I can relate as far as I've heard other stories and seen so many things that happen. And every time you turn on the TV, you hear the awful things that happen to children. I understand it all even though I didn't have a bad childhood. Some of the other issues I understand, but he writes a lot about fighting with your own personal insides. I don't really have things like that going on in my head. I'm pretty at ease with myself and with my life."

On balance, Davis wasn't necessarily aiming to be head spokesperson for the oppressed. There's really a sense that it just kind of happened that way. He was quoted in *Kerrang!* in July 1998; "I don't see myself as doing motivational speeches about childhood traumas... I know I've given a lot of kids strength and they give me strength too. It works back and forth."

And a few months earlier; "People could relate to all that stuff. People like to read about other people's fucking hurts. It's a sick world we're in! So I guess it was good reading for them, but it's my life. I just wanted to be truthful, and at that period of time I was bummed about that shit. And I still am. But at least I have a vehicle to get it out."

'Reclaim My Place' is pure head-banging music with an ambience that lends itself well to any mosh pit. Davis said of the track; "I always do a song about a band member, and this one is about the whole band and how all my life I've been called a homosexual. Even now, I became this big rock star in a band and I'm still called a fag even by my own band. So I was fuckin' pissed off at them. It's like, 'erase them all because I'm gonna reclaim my place and say hey, they owe a lot to me for what I did, and I owe a lot to them back, but, it still kinda sucks.' I've never ever gotten away from that 'fag' fuckin' title. Just because I'm a sensitive kinda guy, and kinda feminine. It really sucks."

Davis said of 'Seed'; "That's all about the same thing again, like in 'Got The Life.' I'm lying in bed in my hotel room or wherever thinking, 'do I really need all this stuff? All this pressure on me?' Because I'm a stressed out freak. The song's about Nathan (Davis' son), it's about how every time that I look into his eyes, I see myself how I used to be, innocent and stress free. I'm jealous of it. It really sucks, I used to be that way. I have to work so hard at this thing in my life. I have to become a stressed-out freak, but I have to put food on the table for my child. Every time I look in his eyes, I just see myself staring right back at my ass laughing. I was care-free, innocent as a child. It's really weird and I'm really jealous of it. That little fucker has my exact same eyes, too. I'm looking at myself when I look at him. It's sad."

Silveria stated that his favourite track on the album was probably 'B.B.K' because "I just like the groove of it." Also Davis said of the track; "That stands for big black cock! That's what I call a Jack and Coke that's served in those little glasses like in Europe. That's what I named it — big black cock. And that's another song about me dealing with the pressures of this album and how I'm trying to kill myself, but, do I really want to kill myself? Things I'm just questioning myself. Like me and myself are just destroying myself with alcohol and everything, because I can't settle everything. But I have decided to get in one of the residential treatment centres that accept private insurance. I'm a really scared little boy."

In the press release, Davis said of 'Cameltosis'; "That's a love song. It's about women in general, women who hurt me. It's Tre's (from The Pharcyde) lyrics. He's going on about chicks, and my chorus is like I'm so scared to love anyone and really let them in after I got hurt really really bad by a girl. I've let Renee (Davis' fiancé at the time) in a little bit, to be honest, but I'll never be that in love ever again. That's what I'm saying, now matter now many times you've loved, once or twice, you're gonna get fucked, 'cause you usually do eventually. The word 'Cameltosis' is a joke. You know, how girls get camel toes when they pull their pants up too high in their crotch? We call it camel toes."

Davis said of 'My Gift To You'; "Renee always wanted me to write her a love song, and that's why I called it 'My Gift To You'. It's my gift to her and you know how I get sick. I always had a fantasy of fucking her and choking her to death. I fantasise about what it would look like through her eyes, with me in her body watching me do it. So it's a really sick, fucked-up song. I did it in the mindset of 'I love her so much, I want to take her out of this world.' It's really strange. She used to leave notes on my pillow with twenty-five ways she'd like to kill me. She's got this weird death fetish. We're kinda fuckin' freaky. She got it. She's all, 'Thank you, that's kinda fucked up. I was expecting a fuckin' 'I love you, baby' kinda song.' I'm all, 'No, you know me. I mean, I can't do that.' I couldn't write a straight love song. I don't know. I put a lot of love into that song, and people were freaked out by it, wondering how I could think like that? But it comes from my upbringing. All that death around me all the time. I've had those sick fuckin' thoughts and I'm not afraid to talk about them. I'm sure everybody's thought about killing themselves. One time I was thinking about it while making love and taking her away from this fuckin' place. I just had the balls to write about it."

During their time at NRG Studios, Korn began to broadcast a weekly *After School Special*. It was a web series of live streams that typically lasted an hour each. It was accessible via RealPlayer every Thursday and it lasted for eight weeks. It featured guest appearances

The Making Of Follow The Leader

from other bands and from stars in the adult entertainment industry as well as Q&A chat and music demos. Quite the achievement considering that in the late nineties, young people's access to the Internet was limited in the days of dialup. The show was a great way for Korn to be able to engage with their audience as well as garner more press interest. This was a perfect vehicle through which Korn were able to get the ball rolling to promote sales of their third album before it was even finished.

Wright was quoted in *The Fader* in August 2018; "We were in the studio six days a week, but we were only really working maybe three days. We had No Work Thursday, which was the Internet broadcast, and then we had Friday — and people couldn't work because it was Friday and they were hungover from No Work Thursday. Then it was Saturday, and you really couldn't do any work. Maybe we got a little bit of guitars done. And then you'd have Sunday off and we'd go back to Monday, and Monday really couldn't work either because 'Oh God, I can't even get out of bed.' Tuesday was a little bit of a workday and Wednesday was used for writing whatever was gonna happen on Thursday, which turned into a big porn party, which, you know. We had special guests in the studio and porn stars because Jonathan was all into that."

Munky was quoted in *The Fader* in August 2018; "Oh my god, that show was so distracting to our process. But then somebody asked us midway through, 'Do you want to stop this?' We were like, 'Hell no, this is fun.'… Dita von Teese came on one of the shows and tied Jonathan up in some weird knot and whipped him. It was awesome."

Silveria said of Korn TV; "I think we just wanted to find out new ways to reach out to Internet users. We had Internet shows for our last record, and they went over really well. We just wanted to take it further, do something even more original and bigger for this next record. I guess we'll figure out more stuff to do on the Internet. Just try to keep everything fresh and new and be one of the leaders."

Davis said in *The Fader* in August 2018; "We pretty much pioneered the whole fucking Internet thing with bands back in the day. We made it into *Time* magazine in 1996. We did the very first webcast — we had Adam Carolla come in to host a show, and we partnered up with Quicktime and they came in and brought all these cameras. 1996 — think about that, technology and the Internet. You could look around in the studio if you dragged a cursor over it. We'd tape songs right off the board and we had little interviews and shit. We really embraced the Internet at the time."

Davis; "We were inspired to do it 'cause of what we did in the past. When we released *Life Is Peachy*, we did *Korn Mangles The Web* with LA Live and that was a two hour long show. With this album, we wanted to do something special, something different, and our manager said that there were these TV-like shows on the web, but a band had never done one. We wanted to do those shows and do it eight times and make it a real TV show with a real TV station since there's no censorship and we could do whatever the fuck we wanted. And we did. And we hope to build it up and make it a company where bands can advertise on our channel and stuff."

Whether the party environment was organised chaos or pure chaos — or a bit of both — is anyone's guess. As well as guest appearances from Marilyn Manson and porn star Ron Jeremy, there were random groupies, drugs and alcohol. It wasn't uncommon for sessions to start at three in the afternoon and run right through into the small hours. There were days when very little work got done. Whilst the party environment was probably enticing for fans and the press to observe, it exacerbated the difficulties that several band members were having with addiction. Head said in *Metal Hammer* in December 2018; "We were twenty five to twenty eight years old, so it was party central. There was a lot of alcohol. Thousands and thousands of dollars! We were out of control! When you party so hard at that age it's a lot of fun, but it was the beginning of a lot of messed up lives… It got pretty crazy, and the fame did go to our heads a little bit and made us a little crazy. Jonathan got suicidal because he was drinking so much Jack and Coke and doing cocaine. He was losing his mind, and he decided to stop it all and get sober during that tour cycle."

Davis once estimated that the bill for alcohol alone was at something over $60,000. Even with many colleagues and passers-by in the studio to enjoy the beer, it was a lot of alcohol. He was quoted in *The Ringer* in August 2018; "That's not even counting the fuckin' drug money I spent on blow."

Munky was quoted in the same feature; "It was fucking crazy. You're giving a bunch of kids money that are already drunks and drug addicts. Probably not the best thing."

So ongoing was the party environment at NRG studios that when 'It's On!' was recorded, Davis refused to sing until he had been given cocaine. As reported in *The Fader* in August 2018; "I refused to start singing unless Toby got me an eight-ball of cocaine right away. Toby started freaking the fuck out, because he knows if I do coke I only get a couple takes and the shit's gonna kick in and then my vocals are going to suck. There was a lot of that."

Whilst this was going on, an orgy was happening elsewhere in the studio. Davis recalled in *The Ringer* in August 2018; "It was the pinnacle of rock and roll excess. I'm singing on a record, I'm high on cocaine, and there's some bitch blowing an amazing fucking musician that's in an amazing band — I'm not naming names, I don't fucking tell. But it was a one of my homies and one of those porn stars. It was amazing."

Coked up or sober whilst doing his vocals, things got wilder when it was time to stop work for the day. Davis relayed in *The Fader* in August 2018; "I'd come in and do my vocals, and once they were done, I'd start drinking. I wasn't drunk when I did my vocals. I was under the influence of some coke at times, but for the majority of it I'd stay sober. Then I was done and I'd just get hammered. We'd start around three or four o' clock, then at nine or ten at night we'd stop and that's when the parties would start. We partied at NRG until four in the morning. Those poor guys would have to leave the place open and we were just raging."

There is a sense that perhaps as their producer, Toby Wright also had to babysit — at least to a point anyway. He was quoted in *The Fader* in August 2018; "I tried to limit the amount of candy that went on before the parts were actually laid down — whether it was beer or weed or whatever. None of it was allowed in the control room. I didn't want to see. I just stayed in the control room and covered my eyes… There's a certain — how do I say it — loveliness to being high while you're playing, and then there's a certain disrespectfulness to your band members and everyone else who's working on your record. You're wasting money and everybody's time."

Munky recalled to *Metal Hammer* in December 2018; "We went in the studio with Steve, and he was going through some personal stuff so he wasn't showing up and wasn't really engaged. The engineer, Toby Wright, took over from that point and helped us engineer and produce the album. But Steve was there when we were doing three or four big songs on the album, and he was a big part of that. And we were fucking around a lot, too. It was chaos! So I can see why somebody would think, 'This is bullshit'."

The party philosophy wasn't new to Korn during the making of the album but certainly, with a bigger budget, things were probably a lot wilder than in the days of making their debut album. Silveria recalled to *Rolling Stone* in December 2014; "On the same piece of property (as the studio) was a cabin that was just an upstairs and a downstairs. The upstairs had four or five beds — like single-sized beds — and the downstairs had the same, that's where everyone slept."

To which Davis chipped in; "It was one big fucking party. Always just out of our minds drunk. By the time it was bedtime, we were just hammered. Staying in the chateau I remember waking up and it was sweltering hot. The sun would just bust through that fucking place. Head took over my vocal booth and he slept in there — he was smart."

Head recalled; "I think I slept in Jon's vocal booth sometimes, and then I slept outside in the drum room. We would get these foam things, the ones that would deaden the sound. I'd put them on the floor, then get blankets and stuff and sleep in there. We were drinking a lot, so I didn't really care about comfort."

Poignantly, Munky said; "At that time, I don't think any of us knew that we were going to have severe addiction problems, so it was all fun at that point."

Fieldy: "You're in the middle of nowhere in the middle of a forest. It's up in these hills and it was a long drive just to get out of there. So you're kind of trapped. And as I learned over the years, they want you to get away from distractions every time we record — but you just find new distractions. We just made a distraction right there. We would bring all our friends up there. We'd have massive parties."

Munky: "We had barbecues every other day. I remember just eating healthy in the afternoon, then partying really hard at night. Ross would have to wrangle us into the studio 'cause we started to get drunk and not really work. But he was good about getting us into the room to record."

Davis: "I was a meth addict when I was doing that fucking record."

Wright was patient though. And it paid off. He was quoted in *The Fader* in August 2018; "It's a matter of just being patient and waiting for the right time. Some people hunt deer and they stand in that darn deer stand until one comes prancing up, and then it's all about that one shot — boom, done. They were patient enough to wait for that one shot. That's what I do with my clients: I wait patiently in the studio for them to have that perfect moment. That's when the magic happens. And there were many magical moments on that record. Munky had a bunch of them. Jonathan had a whole bunch of them... It was a lot of fun, and in the process, we made a record."

Munky said in *Kerrang!* in July 1998; "Once this record comes out, everyone will be excited. The whole band's happy with the record we've made, and I think that's the most important thing."

Silveria stated; "I don't think the production was that different, but the studios were a lot different. We used some of the same equipment, some different equipment which varied in sound. I think since the studio the album was recorded in, and the studio the record was mixed in were different studios, it had a dramatic difference on the way the record came out. That was the main thing on the production. As far as the Korn sound goes and how it turned into new sounds as we went, I don't think that had so much to do with a producer. I think most of it was just writing a record, reflecting on it, then taking all of our thoughts and using them towards the way we want to write the next record. I'm not saying I don't think the producer's ideas were good, whether it be Steve or Ross. I think that they did have something to do with helping the sound, but I don't think they had a tremendous amount to do with the sound. I would credit us very much as far as our sound goes. The biggest difference in recording *Follow The Leader* would probably be Toby and NRG, the studio. As far as the quality of the songs, I wouldn't say they got better because the producers were doing this or that. They helped motivate us. They helped us to keep going if we were getting tired of writing or whatever. I think they helped more in that way rather than actually helping us to form a sound. We just listened to what we did in the past and thought, 'You know, kind of like that. We didn't like that. Let's go more in this direction.' I think we had more to do with it than anybody."

It would be easy to negate the musical merit of *Follow The Leader* based on what was going on in the studio socially when the album was made. The fact remains though that there was a strong extent of creative innovation. To assume that Korn were only in it for the party would be flawed. Head said; "When me and Munky started doing that record, it was about, let's just get guitar pedals out and just get crazy with it. We wanted to make sure the guitar on the noises and the melody parts would sound not so much like the guitar, but like samples, keyboards, or synths."

Munky spoke of his creative rapport with Head in *Total Guitar* in September 1998; "We influence and inspire each other. If I'm having a problem, if I'm in a musical rut, watching Head play inspires me. It is always hard at first, but when our creativity starts sparking, there's no stopping us."

Silveria stated; "Technique-wise, I think I still play the way I always played. I started using D-drum samplers on this record, but I actually ended up not using them as much as I thought I would. I just got a few more shaker sounds and stuff like that. I think the feeling of my playing on the songs is just really fun, and it's the way the songs on this record feel." Upon being asked what advice he would give any aspiring musician, he answered, "Persistence. Try to do the best you can do."

Upon being asked, "What's your favourite new sound or technique that you used for the first time on this album?" Davis stated "I got this voice-bender like a synthesiser. I don't know what it's called, but it does all this weird shit. I used it on this album and I thought it would be cool to hear what I could do with my voice. It worked well. I got all kinds of crazy effects on that thing. I use it on almost the whole album. It makes my voice lower, makes it sound like I'm in a megaphone, it doubles my voice, makes it sound like I have a wah-wah on my voice. It does all kinds of things."

Besides, what's a bit of partying if it gives an artist a free-range environment in which to create? Davis said in *Kerrang!* in March 1998; "I need distractions. I don't start writing 'til' fucking midnight or one in the morning. So I party on or whatever, then I come back all drunk and write. It's the most vulnerable time for me, when I can sit down and work. I can search my fucking head for stuff. With me, it's a total channelling thing. When I write lyrics it's like 'Boom!' —I'm getting my inspiration from somewhere else. Sometimes when I'm drunk I fucking flow. But I can do that when I'm sober too."

He recalled to *The Ringer* in August 2018; "It was just partying and doing shit to inspire us. We weren't thinking, 'Oh, this needs to be a single.' That's one thing I love about our band. We just wrote the songs and handed it to the label, 'Here you go, take it or leave it'."

'Got The Life' was awarded gold certification in Australia by the Australian Recording Industry Association. It peaked at number one on the Canadian RPM Rock/Alternative chart. It also got to number fifteen on the US Billboard Mainstream Rock Tracks chart and number seventeen on the US Billboard Modern Rock Tracks chart.

The single was sent to radio stations on July 24th 1998, and has been released five times. It was first released was on August 10th 1998 whereby there were two different version in the US. The single included different mixes of the song, including 'Deejay Punk-Roc Remix' and 'D.O.S.E.'s Woollyback Remix'.

The second version of the single is backed with 'I Can Remember' and 'Good God (OOMPH! vs. Such A Surge Remix)'. 'Got The Life' was also released as a single in Australia, and in the United Kingdom twice. At three minutes and forty-five seconds long, 'Got The Life' is the shortest song on the album. 'Got The Life (Deejay Punk-Roc remix)' was mixed by Deejay Punk-Roc and Jon Paul Davies, and was recorded at Airdog Funk Research Department and Liverpool,

England.

'D.O.S.E.'s Woollyback Remix' was mixed by D.O.S.E. in courtesy of Mercury Records. Korn hired McG to direct the video for 'Got The Life'. He had already worked on other videos for songs from their first album: 'Blind', 'Shoots And Ladders', 'Clown' and 'Faget'.

For the video of 'Freak On A Leash', Korn brought in the talents of Todd McFarlane. It was a natural choice what with McFarlane already having designed the album's cover. Davis said; "I really fuckin' liked his art when I saw *Spawn*. That shit's just scary. And I thought it would go along great with us. And Todd never did any album covers. He had great big fuckin' offers from Metallica, Marilyn Manson, and he thought that we were like The Doors of the nineties. So he was totally into it, and we thought that it would be a good idea. So Fieldy came up with the concept of the children jumping off a cliff. It was really cool. We really dug it. My friend Sean is the one who initially drew some pictures of the hopscotch thing, and he totally fuckin' turned it around and made it look fucked up. All these little Korn children, 'children of the Korn', jumping down off the cliff onto the earth, which is below them, like they're just jumping off the cliff onto the earth, losing their innocence and becoming fucked like all of us. In a sense, it's the doom of living I guess. So Sean sketched out that idea up for us and then Todd ran with it. The cover continues that theme that Korn has on every album. There are always images of children and the fucked-up-ness is always there. Because innocence is fuckin' scary. It leaves a big fuckin' space for your mind to go off. It's really scary. Children are always scared when they're all happy and stuff. They're the most beautiful thing in the world, but when you see it in our artwork, the way we've placed it, it's just kinda fuckin' weird. It makes you think a lot."

Fieldy said in *Kerrang!* in January 1999; "The concept was more about something our Moms would say when we were kids. When you're ten, out playing with your friends and some of them are doing drugs or whatever, you go home and she's like 'if they jumped of a cliff, would you follow them?!'."

The album's artwork was certainly iconic. It was reported in

The Making Of Follow The Leader

Billboard in July 1998; "Another special element of *Follow The Leader* is the album art... Limited edition lithographs (signed by the band and McFarlane) of the artwork will be given away via radio and retail promotions."

McFarlane had worked as part of a team with Dayton & Faris before, who had already made videos for R.E.M. and the Smashing Pumpkins. Silveria explained; "We had heard from Al Masocco (Epic VP of Marketing) that Todd had actually referred to us as 'The Doors of the nineties' and it got everyone really excited. So after we were asked to do the *Spawn* soundtrack and we had seen his art, we knew what he was capable of. Al came back and asked us if we were interested in working with him more. Then we approached Todd to do our album cover and he seemed really enthusiastic about it. We were really excited and everyone was surprised that he was anxious to work with us as we hoped he would be. I guess we didn't think he would be into it that much, doing the album cover, but he came back to us right away saying he would love to do it. We were blown away. We didn't think this guy would want to work with us as much and like the band that much."

In terms of the technology available at the time, the video for 'Freak On A Leash' was considered to be groundbreaking — so much so that the use of bullet-time special effects would go on to be an iconic aspect of the film, *The Matrix* (which was released the following year).

Davis said in *The Fader* in August 2018; "It felt like when someone read the fucking script for *The Matrix* for the first time: 'Are you kidding me? This can't be done.'... We went home, went on tour, and they beamed it to us in Australia after they got all these special effects done. We saw it and I was like, 'Oh my god, this is fucking pretty brilliant. I ain't never seen no shit like this'."

Video directors, Jonathan Dayton and Valerie Faris said; "It's a perfect music video song — like a movie soundtrack. There's so much tension in the opening verses, and it just keeps building until the whole thing explodes in that final bridge. Our favourite part is when Jonathan yells 'Go!' and the bullet reverses direction. The structure of the song became our script, and it was clear what we had to do. We suggested the concept of having a bullet leave the animated world and travel through the real world until it finally returns again to the poster... It was inspired by high-speed still photography where a bullet shoots through an apple. It was so fun to work on. We shot real bullets through all the objects, and most of the "effects" are real. All the bullets were fired on a closed shooting range and then put into locations."

Munky said; "They explained, 'We'll shoot a bunch of this, we'll have you guys, and then we're gonna tie it in with Todd McFarlane's animation in the beginning.' We were like, 'Holy shit, if you can pull this off with this song, it's gonna be a fucking home run.' We were blown away... We didn't really understand how they made it. Even just trying to imagine Jonathan staring at an animated bullet was just like, 'What? Really? You want me to pretend there's a bullet right here and I'm looking at it?'."

Fieldy recalled; "Today, people do that in three minutes on their laptops. But back then, nobody."

Head: "It was surreal being at that level back then, which is unheard of now: a video budget of $800,000, or whatever it ended up being. it was crazy."

The video for 'Freak On A Leash' exceeded expectations when it became number one on MTV's *Total Live Request* on 25th February 1999. This is all the more impressive considering that it sat alongside Britney Spears' 'Baby One More Time' and NSYNC's 'A Little More Time On You'.

Before eventually retiring 'Freak On A Leash', MTV had begun showing only snippets of the video. It is considered by some that this was on account of pressure from parental groups. A lot of parents didn't like Korn and their music. Upon being asked, "How do you feel about all these parents that have come out and condemned you for your music? They don't realise that they've actually created the problems Korn sing about", Davis replied; "I know. They're the ones that did it. We gotta thank the parents for doing that to kids. It's like thanks for making our lives hell. Because of you, we're here."

The 'Freak On A Leash' video was awarded Best Editing and Best Rock Video at the MTV awards. It also won a Grammy for

The Making Of Follow The Leader

Best Short Form Music Video. Dayton and Faris said; "We loved the response, Korn fans are so loyal. We still get people telling us how much they love the video."

It could be said that the success of *Follow The Leader* was such that the video for 'Freak On A Leash' was highly anticipated even before it was released. MTV News reported in December 1998 "Korn To Mix Animation And Live Footage For New Video: As Korn prepares to wind down its post-Family Values tour with a concert at Los Angeles' Shrine Auditorium on Friday, the band is getting ready to film its long-awaited second video. Korn will be shooting the clip for its next single, 'Freak On A Leash', on December 13th and 14th in LA with *Spawn* creator Todd McFarlane, along with the directorial team of Jonathan Dayton and Valerie Faris. Plans currently call for the video to be a mixture of animation and live performance footage, a move which harkens back to McFarlane's last video credit, as he helmed the fully-animated video for Pearl Jam's 'Do The Evolution'. The renowned comic-book artist also created the cover art for Korn's current album, *Follow The Leader*. The directing duo of Dayton and Faris have won more than their fair share of Video Music Awards for their work, which includes videos for the Smashing Pumpkins, Scott Weiland and Neil Finn. Korn's video for 'Freak On A Leash' is expected to start airing on MTV in late January."

Indeed, as the video's release date loomed ever closer, MTV keenly reported in February 1999; "Korn 'Freak' Video To Debut On Friday: Three directors and many special effects later, Korn is finally ready to unveil the second video from its *Follow The Leader* album. The band will roll out its latest clip, 'Freak On A Leash', Friday on MTV's *Total Request Live* at 3:30pm. As we first reported in December of last year, the band hooked up with *Spawn* creator Todd McFarlane and the award-winning video directing team of Jonathan Dayton and Valerie Faris this time around. The clip mixes animation with live action and gives all involved the chance to flaunt their strengths. McFarlane twists an animated adventure around the children he created for the *Follow The Leader* cover art, while Dayton and Faris combine special effects and clever camera moves in the live action portion of the video. To reveal any more would be to give away twists and turns crucial to the clip but rest assured that there is plenty of Korn performance footage as well."

Impressively, 'Freak On A Leash' was one of the first songs that Korn penned when preparing to record the album. Munky said in August 2018; "It was one of the first tracks we wrote for that album."

Ironically, as commercially successful as the song was, it was actually anti music industry. Davis said; "That's my song that rails out against the music industry. It's about how I feel like I'm a fuckin' prostitute. Like I'm this freak paraded around, but I got corporate America fuckin' making all the money while it's taking a part of me. It's like they stole something from me — they stole my innocence and I'm not calm anymore. I worry constantly. I'm not just talkin' about the record business. Everything's involved. I've lost something. I'm not all there anymore. I love what I do, but I wish I could have it all back. It's like the Peter Pan syndrome. I wish I could still fly."

He was quoted in *New Musical Express* in September 1998; "You're just a fucking product. We're just fucking pimped by the record company. We're just paraded around but they made all the money. They sit back and reap the benefits of it and we go through all sorts of hell."

To which Silveria was quoted, "I guess we're about $1500 a night whores."

With hindsight on his side, Davis explained in 2018 what 'Freak On A Leash' is about; "The music industry, entertainment in general — how the machine worked. The label, management, publishers, everything that it involved. Looking back on it, 'something takes a part of me' was about how they were taking the fun out of making music and making it a business. You can ask anyone in my band, I hate the fucking music industry — I don't give a fuck. I love singing and I love fucking making music and I don't care about shit I don't care about. I know it's stupid, but this is how I roll. It was me lashing out, because when we started getting bigger after *Life Is Peachy* and got a bigger budget, I was watching it become more of a business — gotta do this, gotta do that."

'Freak On A Leash' wasn't written with commerciality in mind. It was reported in *Spin* in November 1998; "Ambition flowing,

The Making Of Follow The Leader

conversation turns to the selection of the album's second single. 'Freak On A Leash' is a band favourite and a logical choice, but there's a noisy guitar break in the middle, and radio hates noisy guitar breaks. It's during moments like these — stay true or sell out? our way or the highway? — that legends are born."

Whilst an amount of the lyrical content in *Follow The Leader* is just as macabre as Korn's previous two albums, the subject matters explored shifted more towards what was relevant to Davis' frame of reference at the time. Davis was quoted in *Metal Hammer* in January 2019; "*Follow The Leader* is my album of self-destruction. There's none of my childhood stuff going on any more. This is more about me dealing with pressures I put on myself. The pressure of what it's like to be in this band, of being a father, all kinds of shit."

Davis stated; "My thoughts going into this record were that I've already sung two albums of just straight fuckin' cathartic rage. To keep myself real and to keep my integrity, I gotta move on. I mean, there are only so many things in my life I can scream about. It's getting ridiculous. I want to keep that going and become a better singer. I've always wanted to be a true singer. I think on this album I finally became a singer and I still got across with my melodies what I was feeling. To me, melodies are more fucking intense than a scream. If it's such an intense melody, I feel it even more. It just takes me somewhere. It's spiritual. That's all I wanted to do on this album. It's time for me to move on. I don't want to stay the same or take a step down. I just want to move on and do something exciting and new and make people go, 'Fuck'."

As well as lyrically, *Follow The Leader* was a step up musically. Munky said in an interview on KLOS 95.5 with DJ Full Metal Jackie in June 2018; "It was fun but really, it was trying to figure out, 'okay, we kind of did these two angst records. Let's move into more of a song based, lightened mood. Let's have fun a little bit.' That's when we really started to kind of find who we were and make changes as far as song structures and listening to each other play. Like, 'Man, you're really good. I didn't realise it before'."

Silveria stated; "We were hoping to write and record the best record we could. We didn't want to make it sound like the first or second record, but we wanted to keep it sounding like Korn. We wanted to take the songs to a new level even with somewhat of a new writing style. We just basically wanted to make a good record, one we were happy with, something that sounded like it took a step up from the first two records."

Could Korn have finished making *Follow The Leader* sooner? Well, possibly. But as Munky was quoted in *Kerrang!* in July 1998; "We tried not to give ourselves a schedule. We had to take as much time as we needed."

To which Davis added, "Of course, the record company and the management had a schedule, but we kept fucking breaking it."

Munky told *The Fader* in 2018; "We probably could have sped things up and had more focus — that's sort of the beauty of it though. There wasn't one direction." Agreeably, the album is very much of its time in terms of where Korn were at as a band. Wright said in 2018; "We probably wasted a lot of time experimenting, but I don't think experiments are a waste of time at all. You get something very unique and something that not everybody has."

Silveria stated; "We sit in a rehearsal studio, set up recording equipment and we meet everyday. Unless someone has an idea they thought of at home or something, we pretty much sit down with our instruments and start trying ideas. As far as the Korn sound goes, it's just what we like — it was not preconceived that we have to write like this and make every song like this. We try anything and if we like it, we use it. It's pretty much simple as that. There was not a lot of thought behind the creative direction, and we didn't say that we have to stay on this direction — it's music we like and the way we write the songs."

Davis said; "Our only goal was to take our time on this album because I knew we had it in us that we could do something great, fully integrate both albums and put out an album that we could really be proud of. Because, shit! The first album only took four months to write, record and mix. This one took nine, so that was our attitude and we wanted to do some phat shit."

Billboard considered of the album in May 2002; "The band took its time to ensure that this album would benefit from the success of

The Making Of Follow The Leader

the previous ones, giving *Follow The Leader* a crisp, higher quality sound."

Prior to doing their own touring to promote *Follow The Leader*, Korn were actually due to play at the Ozzfest in Milton Keynes in the UK. There are conflicting accounts as to how official that was and how it came to be that the plan fell through but either way, the time that the band spent on finishing the album was such that it would have been asking a lot of their schedule anyway.

Davis told *Kerrang!* in July 1998; "We wouldn't have been able to play the Ozzfest anyway, because we were running over time on the mix."

Munky added; "We took nine months to do this record and we wanted to finish it right." It was asserted in *Kerrang!* in January 1999; "Predictably, Korn's non-appearance at last year's Ozzfest tops The Shittiest Thing Of '98 category." To which Fieldy was quoted; "What sucks is, we never said we were gonna play those shows. We said 'We want to play, but we're not sure what our schedule's like.' Next thing we knew, there were ads up saying we were playing. We were like 'What the fuck?!' We never confirmed it... We'll be back to the UK to do a bigger, better and longer show. As soon as possible. That's all we can do... Any Korn fan will know our favourite audiences are in Europe and the UK. We even say that the American crowds suck and need to pay attention to the European crowds! All of Europe puts 'em to shame."

Ultimately, it comes across that it was family stuff that accounted for Korn opting out of doing the Ozzfest. Davis said in *Kerrang!* in July 1998; "Basically, it was all set up, then Head was like, 'Shit! When's that Ozzfest?!' We were like 'Oh fuck!' For a while, he (Head) kept changing his mind about whether or not to do it... So yeah, this kind of stretched out. Finally we told him, 'Man, there's gonna be tons of Ozzfests and only one time when your child's born.' If he wasn't there, he'd be fucked for the rest of his life because she'd say 'You weren't there'."

Upon being asked why they didn't just get another guitarist in to be able to do the Ozzfest, Davis was quoted in the same feature; "Korn's the five of us. We're never gonna have no replacements... We're family, man. Part of the magic of Korn is all five of us. Without

Head there, I'd look over and freak out."

To which Munky was quoted, "I couldn't throw my beer bottle at a complete stranger."

Upon being asked if they got shit from Ozzy's management, Davis was quoted in *Kerrang!* in July 1998; "We always get shit from 'em! But I like Sharon Osbourne. We made up. Everything's cool. Our management was scared to tell Sharon because they'd just got off the phone from telling her Limp Bizkit had pulled out." (to clarify, Munky was quoted, "Us and Bizkit have the same management team.").

****

Follow The Leader was reviewed in *Rolling Stone* in August 1998; "Anger is not pretty or pleasant. It can turn violent, hurtful, even homicidal. But there are times when just getting mad beats getting even, when that backlog of rage, resentment and helplessness is something to be exorcised — channelled to a purifying extreme that leaves you feeling scrubbed raw and new. And Korn know where that's at. In *Follow The Leader*, vocalist Jonathan Davis, bassist Reggie "Fieldy" Arvizu, guitarists James "Munky" Shaffer and Brian "Head" Welch, and drummer David Silveria have made an ideal record for those long, black days when all you can do is stand up and scream, 'What the fuck! What the fuck! What the fuck!' at bloody-murder volume. Which is exactly what Davis does at the end of 'Reclaim My Place', starting in a flat, blank whisper over the isolated gurgle of Munky's guitar. Then Davis pumps up the vigour. His chanting escalates into giddy, visceral, singsong confusion as the ruckus around him — the dentist-drill whine and power-chord fisticuffs of Shaffer's and Welch's guitars, the vicious slap of Silveria's snare drum — rips into last-ditch overdrive. Davis is not working a wide range of vocabulary or metaphor here. In general, as a singer and lyricist, he prefers direct accusation — 'You really want me to be a good son/Why you make me feel like no one?' ('Dead Bodies Everywhere') — and caged-animal babble (the Busta

The Making Of Follow The Leader

Rhymes-in-Bellevue outburst in 'Freak On A Leash') to reasoned discourse. But for Korn, the maelstrom is the message. And in a thin-fun year of bilge-water soundtrack albums and glucose-shock R&B, 'Reclaim My Place' is top infernorock theatre and one of the reasons why *Follow The Leader*, Korn's third album, will be the late '98 toast of Skateboard Nation. In attack and distemper, Korn have the nineties hip-hop, amp-death aesthetic — NIN meet N.W.A.; Rollins Against the Machine — down to ferocious perfection. 'Children Of The Korn' is an emergency-transmission mélange of brittle machine beats, densely packed guitar distortion and the tandem barking of Davis ('All I want to do is live!') and special guest Ice Cube ('Stop fuckin' wit' me!'). A smart, sharp example of Korn's style of modular writing, 'Seed' is two mind games in one: big chunks of death march funk and opaque stretches of echoey dub in which the guitars sound as though they're broadcasting from a watery grave. *Follow The Leader* is also true to an older, vital hard-rock tradition of cleansing brutality and transcendent guitar choler — Blue Cheer's 1968 speed freak's delight, *Vincebus Eruptum*; early Metallica and very early Black Sabbath; the molten heave 'n' thump of Funkadelic's *Cosmic Slop*; the claustrophobic fury of Steve Albini's mid-eighties band Big Black."

The review continued, "It may be the fact that Shaffer and Welch both play seven-string guitars, but there is an extra, weighty abrasion to their riffing that, at full throttle, seems to cleave the music in half, pressing everything else in the mix toward the margins. Silveria's bona fide disco beat is the sucker bait in 'Got The Life', but it's the crisp crush of bass-and-dual-guitar menace that makes the track fat with tension. When the band abruptly switches from the cold, clipped chorus of 'It's On' to the bright, Big Chord bridge, it's as if Korn have suddenly stepped out of their angst bunker into A-bomb-white daylight. 'Pretty', though, is a point at which *Follow The Leader* takes a giant step past profane invective and impressive guitar pyro. As a teenager, Davis worked as an autopsy assistant in a Bakersfield, California, coroner's office, and 'Pretty' is based on the particularly heinous case of a twelve-month-old rape victim. Against a jarring mix of goth like ballad murk and a blowout hook in which the guitars seem to be reduced to pure static, Davis doesn't flinch from the horror, looking straight at the battered body, chewing hard on his words. And in the chorus — 'I see a pretty face/Smashed against the bathroom floor/What a disgrace/Who do I feel sorry for?' — Davis honestly testifies to his own trauma, to seeing in that toddler's body the bleak prospect of being left behind in a world capable of such unspeakable evil. Davis has already taken hard, fierce looks at child abuse and dysfunctional family values on Korn's previous albums: 'Daddy', on 1994's *Korn*, and 'Kill You', on 1996's *Life Is Peachy* (not!). But in 'Pretty', Davis' outrage and the torrid guitar drama fuse to a vivid, lethal degree. It's too bad that Korn can go so easily from the potent to the pointless. The very next track, 'All In The Family', is an MC duel between Davis and Fred Durst of Limp Bizkit, a stomping hip-hop track with a good-natured barrage of insults — except for the 'faggot' and 'fairy' cracks and lame-o lines like 'Suck my dick, kid, like your daddy did' and 'You're a fag and on a lower level.' To Davis and Durst, that may just be harmless schoolyard jivin'. But Davis knows words can hurt — that was the whole point of 'Faget' on *Korn* — and the homosexual slams in 'All In The Family' cheapen, at least for those five minutes, the power and integrity of an album otherwise devoted to kickin' it against cruelty and prejudice. Korn's only other problem is timing; they've released their best album just as alternative punk-funk-metal whatever is in commercial and creative eclipse. It is easy to hear in *Follow The Leader* the last great roar of a once-good idea. It is also easy, from a music-biz perch, to misread and underestimate the needs and loyalties of Young Pissed-off America. Either way, *Follow The Leader* is going to blow up in your face. Prepare to eat shrapnel — whether you like it or not."

It was reviewed in *Spin* in October 1998; "For millions of kids, Korn's house of pain feels like a home away from home. Korn must surely be the only band ever to distribute a press kit that announces 'several members have experienced the catastrophic effects of child abuse.' That announcement is also easily the biggest 'duh!' in Korn's whole press kit. Listen to *Follow The Leader* and you know this band is damaged goods. Korn try to scream their way out of a black-and-blue bedroom, with words that level blame and thudding queasy riffs that try to even the score. And they still can't break free. At a time when

The Making Of Follow The Leader

"protecting children" has become the motor powering a nationwide moral panic, when teenage cafeteria killers get massive coverage, and when every politico's pet peeve — tobacco, crime, Internet porn, you name it — is sold to the public as a way of safeguarding the young, Korn must be the most political band in the country. Their music has scared the shit out of highschool administrators, and you can hear the Christian righteous warning America from the pulpit: Don't let your kids become children of the Korn. The band's first two albums went platinum without support from radio or MTV, and *Follow The Leader*, sleeker and more focused, seems sure to follow. All of which indicates that far from being locked in his room alone with his wretched feelings, Korn singer Jonathan Davis has plenty of company. Calling Korn the most political band around is precisely the kind of thing that would have the band themselves reaching for more ice coldies, then belching en masse. They don't really believe in anything themselves, other than that when your head hits the 7-Eleven parking lot, it really hurts, man. On *Follow The Leader* Korn even cover Cheech & Chong's invincible 'Earache My Eye' (cameo by Cheech Marin) yet they aren't really part of the fart-lighting *South Park* nation. Even when they try to be funny, Korn are pathetic, and I mean that in sort of a good way — they can't help but show you what torn-up sock puppets they are. For all their ugly lashing out at targets that have regularly included women and 'faggots,' they radiate more pain than hate, the kind of pain they never got over. 'Dead Bodies Everywhere' opens with music box tinkling, then plows into dumbed-down Rage Against The Machine slab guitar and bass-popping."

The review continued, "Korn use haunted-house minor chords and guitar strings that squeal like Theremins to give their child abuse lyrics the feel of slasher flicks. And if they identify with the stalker, they always cast themselves as the ultimate victims. 'I see a pretty face, smashed against the bathroom floor/What a disgrace, who do I feel sorry for?' Davis says on 'Pretty'. The answer to that one is easy: He feels sorry for himself. When Rage Against The Machine, the band Korn most resembles, borrow from hip-hop, it's a multicultural gesture that rocks like Everest. But Korn are, ahem, post-PC: They see foul-mouthed, brawling rappers as expressing ultimate taboos, and they feel right at home. For Korn (and their buds Limp Bizkit) hip-hop's noise won't save the world, but it keeps the victims from going bonkers. On 96's *Life Is Peachy* they covered Ice Cube's 'Wicked', and Cube returns the favour by guesting on 'Children Of The Korn'. Elsewhere Pharcyde's Tre works out on 'Cameltosis', and Davis and Bizkit's Fred Durst attempt a hip-hop "battle". But for all the breakbeats that cool the molten guitar, Korn are, in the end, a million miles from Compton. They are, in fact, from Bakersfield, West Coast hillbilly music mecca. Davis' dad was even a member of Buck Owens' Buckaroos, and Radio Korn, as it happens, was the hillbilly station on a regular *Hee Haw* sketch. Korn are unmistakably referencing personal torture, but they haven't figured out what to do with abuse except visit it on others. And so the incest, the boozing, the rage against God and the beatin' of their women all end up seeming like nothing but one more dumbass hillbilly parody. They've raised a bumper crop of Korn nuts in the way Metallica and underground rappers did, by mattering at a strictly word-of-mouth level. Korn scare all the right people — critics and faculty — but resonance is only supposed to be a beginning, not an end in itself. They don't have to grow up, they don't have to achieve "closure", but if they're not going to make good records, what's the point of going through all of that therapy?"

In a press release for *Follow The Leader*, upon being asked to describe his life in five words, Davis said "I'm stressed out — and comfortable." And in response to being asked what advice he would give to aspiring musicians, his reply was a succinct one of "turn back."

The *Rocky Mountain News* considered in September 1998; "For the uninitiated, the classic Korn sound comes rumbling out of the speakers on the first cut. 'It's On!' grinds fuzzy guitars, thunderous beats and shouts of gut-wrenching rage into an anthem for the alienated... How far can growling, guttural blasts of hatred and anger take a band? In Korn's case, all the way to number one, where the quintet's latest album, the aptly titled *Follow The Leader*, was perched one week after its release."

Having made an impact with the album itself, it was time to take things on the road.

Chapter Three
Touring And Making An Impact

Munky was quoted in *Guitarist* in October 1998; "Heavy metal isn't as big as it used to be, but I think we're creating something new anyway — a unique sound that's moving the whole rock scene forward."

Due to the financial support that Korn had behind them from the record label, with the release of *Follow The Leader* came a large scale promotional project. In an innovative PR strategy, the band embarked on the Korn Kampaign whereby they travelled from town to town to meet and greet fans at various record stores across America. No expense was spared when it came to modes of transport, which included a private jet and a tank.

Davis said to *The Fader* in August 2018; "Labels would invest in bands. You could do crazy-ass shit. The shit that we pulled off back in the day — we hired a fucking private jet, flew around the United States, and did two in-stores a day. We signed five to ten thousand albums a day. We were fucking beat: start in the morning, go to one city for five hours, jump in the plane, do the next one, do another five fucking hours, go to bed, jump on the plane."

Munky was quoted in the same feature; "The only way we did it was because they said 'private jet.' So we were like, 'Fuck yeah! A jet, I'll go anywhere!'."

Head: "One of my best memories was going down the streets of Canada on an army tank. These fans were just running after us like, 'Hey you guys rule!' We'd give them peace signs on top of this tank and end up at the record store. Nothing cooler than that."

The Korn Kampaign was hosted by Jim Rose, who had recently risen to fame as a sideshow host and performer at Lollapalooza. A natural showman, he was able to get the attention of a crowd when it mattered. Rose said in 2018; "I created the vibe that allowed the reveal — whatever it was — keeping the crowd entertained and hyping how great Korn and this album is. It was never the same in any city, a lot of organising for each event. These guys exploded right in front of me. It was a different kind of vibe, man. They just showed up like Vikings, went from city to city, and ripped them apart."

Cynically, a reporter considered of the Korn Kampaign in *New Musical Express* in September 1998; "You've got to wonder what Korn have got that makes five thousand plus kids, most of whom regard Nirvana and Metallica as ancient history, stand all day baking in sunshine for the ever-diminishing chance of a quick handshake, snatched photo, a smile and an autograph. And you've also got to wonder what drives Korn to sit there smiling and scribbling and saying 'no dude, *you* rock!' again and again for hour after hour, day after day."

Not only were Korn promoting themselves, but other artists whose work they believed in. It was reported in *Billboard* in October 1998; "In Epic's promotion with Korn, customers who brought the act's *Follow The Leader* at Best Buy outlets, as well as at independent stores, received a free compilation CD containing songs from other hard rock acts."

Korn picked the acts that would go on the CD. In March 2000, *Billboard* estimated that about 100,000 copies of the sampler CD were given out with the purchase of *Follow The Leader*. The CD featured up and coming artists including Kid Rock, Orgy and Limp Bizkit.

Korn's career had begun picking up tremendous momentum. Epic organised a promotional event that was to take place at Tower Records in Manhattan. Davis was unable to attend due to the fact that his grandfather had just passed away, something that further intensified his poor mental health at the time. For the event, traffic was brought to a standstill due to around nine thousand fans making their way to meet their heroes.

Davis said to *The Ringer* in August 2018; "The police literally picked (the band) up and drove them out of Manhattan and said,

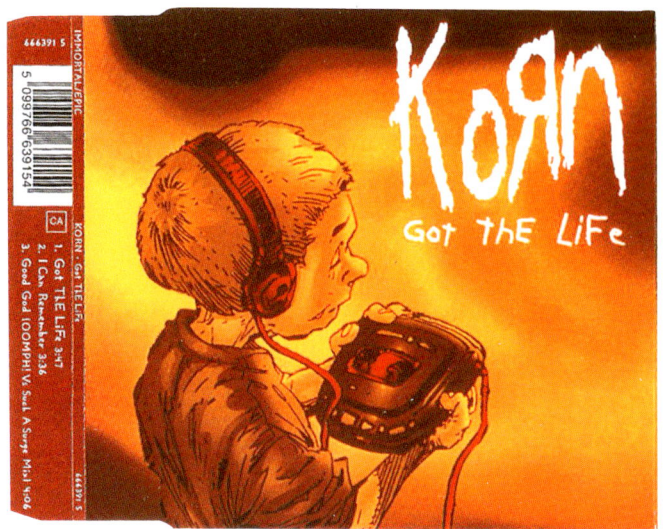

CD singles were released from the album, in multiple formats. The group shot version is European and includes three different mixes of the track as well as a 'Children Of The Korn (Clarkworld Remix)'.

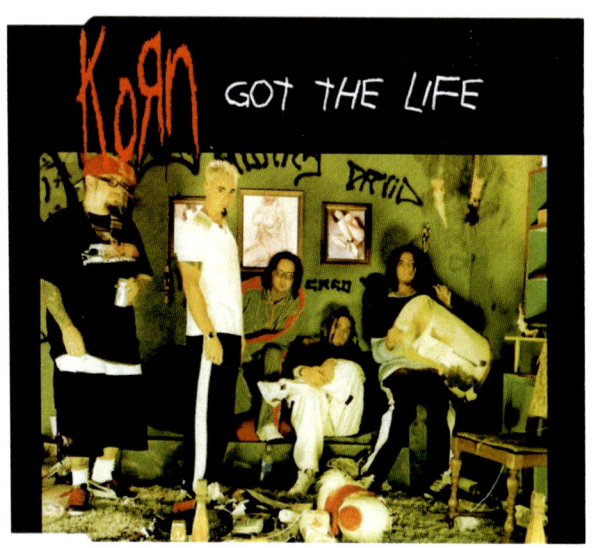

A 12" single of 'Got The Life' was also released in Europe.

As with 'Got The Life' there were multiple versions of 'Freak On A Leash' singles, including a numbered limited edition released in the UK.

In the UK a limited edition, numbered, 12" single was also released.

The album's sleeve design was pretty well used universally although as is always the case, the Japanese version had a wrap around obi strip.

In the UK there was a special boxed set edition known as The Quorn Box. It included two CD singles, stickers and a T-Shirt and was a limited edition of 2,000 copies.

The album was also released on double vinyl and cassette.

As a sign of the album's durability, it has been frequently reissued. The CD here was a German only digipack release.
    With the advent of a renaissance in vinyl the album has also seen numerous LP reissues including this one on clear vinyl.

'Don't come back.' It was like being in the fuckin' Beatles or some shit. That's when we were like, 'okay, we're a fuckin' big band now'."

He was quoted in *Melody Maker* in May 1999; "I was on the Korn Kampaign and my grandfather died. I was having bad panic attacks then and I thought, 'I'm gonna quit drinking, I'm gonna get my life together, I'm gonna start taking my medicine, I can't live like this.' Because I wanted to kill myself, I slipped so down in depression I wanted to die. I didn't want to wake up in the morning. And it scared me, man. I didn't take pills or slit my wrists but I was thinking about it... but I'm still scared to die forever. It was part of my panic. I wanna live to be old. I don't mind growing old. But I wanna fucking kick ass while I'm young now... They got me on Prozac. I started taking it six months ago. I had to wean myself on it with a child's dosage and I take it in liquid form because I don't like pills. It makes me happy and normal. I can handle things now. And I can go out to bars and party. Because I don't drink, I say I'm always partying. I like hanging out where everybody's drunk and I just laugh. It's really, really cool, man. Alcohol's such a depressant... I wish I could drink. I remember how it feels. It's fun. But when I was drunk, I could be myself, I'd lose all inhibitions and a wall would come down. Now, by being sober, I can tear down that wall myself. I can do what I want and not be scared. I always feel so fragile. Insecure. And I've had enough of that shit."

****

Whilst Korn were confident that they had made a good album and did have high hopes for it, they didn't anticipate quite how big it would be. It exceeded their expectations commercially as well as personally. Head was quoted in *Metal Hammer* in December 2018; "I was in a record store signing records. I don't remember the city, but I called my dad, like, 'Dad, we went to number one!' He was always the type who was telling me to cut my hair, so he got to a place where he was like, 'Man, I was wrong about you. I should have just let you be you.' That was really cool of him to say."

September 1998 saw the Family Values tour take off on the road.

Korn - *Follow The Leader*: In-depth

In tow with Korn were Limp Bizkit, Ice Cube, Orgy and Rammstein. It was a fantastic opportunity for everyone to raise their profile. Running until late October 1998, the Family Values tour grossed over $6.4 million dollars. By keeping ticket prices low (typically below thirty dollars), the gigs were made accessible to a wide audience and went in favour of Korn's image of being "for the fans".

Tactical move or a heartfelt one, it made business sense considering Korn's appeal to a young audience. The success of the tour was such that is was considered to be a major factor in drastically increasing sales of *Follow The Leader*. Regarding how the Family Values tour came to be, Silveria explained; "We saw other festival type tours out there and there really weren't any of them we wanted to be on. So we thought, 'why don't we try putting together our own festival and we can pick the bands and determine the vibe of the festival and how it's run and where we go with it?' We thought we would give it a shot. So, we got some partners together to help us with it and started creating the tour. We put everyone's ideas in a pot and started writing out a map for it. It actually ended up being really good, and we thought we could do something better than what was out there."

Fieldy was quoted of the idea behind the Family Values tour in *Billboard* in July 1998; "It started out over the years from going to Lollapalooza, and there'd be like one band you want to see and you had to sit through all these shitty bands to get to it. So we decided to put on our own tour with five or so bands that everyone would like."

Davis said; "It was the brainchild of Jeff (Kwatinetz, Korn's manager), thinking that we could do this thing right because we saw what happened with Lollapalooza, putting shitty bands together and it not really working out. We wanted something that was really pumpin' with something new, something that had spark to it. We really wanted something special, so we got the idea for Family Values to put together all the up-and-coming heavy bands. We did it and let's rock! I don't know how far off into the future we'll have it. Personally, I'd like to see it go out three or four times and then we'll probably just end it because by then, it will probably just burn out. That's what happened to Lollapalooza. But I'd like to have it go out a good four times — as long as there's good, new music coming out."

It was reported in *Soundbites* in March 1998; "After touring with last year's disappointing Lollapalooza, Southern California heavies Korn have decided to launch Family Values, their very own travelling festival. No headliners are yet confirmed for the inaugural run this summer, but Korn's wish list includes the Deftones, Limp Bizkit, and Helmet. 'We're going to cash in on the hard music major-label execs think doesn't sell', says vocalist Jonathan Davis, adding that Korn recently started a hard-rock record label named Elementree. But the band is most concerned with finishing their third album, which is set for a spring release. 'It's groovier and harder and I sing a lot more', says Davis 'We're now in a position to make something we're really proud of'."

Davis added; "I think the current state of music sucks. There are only a few bands that are worth a shit out there: Deftones, Limp Bizkit and us. And, now there's Orgy and Videodrone, but I'm saying for us, as far as our kind of music, I think it really is sad that we're the only good thing that's come around in the nineties, anything heavy. It seems like everything went soft, and I think that Korn is contributing to it by creating a new style of music and bringing heavy music back, putting the "rock" back in "rock & roll" 'cause it seems like it's gotten really stale. Bands are just too 'la la la' and happy now. There's no fun in it anymore, it lost its fun. I think that the only cool thing that came out of the nineties is Limp Bizkit, Deftones and us."

From smaller gigs to regularly playing large arenas, it was a whole new ball game and certainly took some getting used to. *Kerrang!* advocated in January 1999; "1998 was the year when Korn became genuine arena killers."

Davis said in 2018; "We were put right into arenas (for the Family Values tour). I quit drinking, so I was detoxing the whole fucking tour. I was going insane and had horrible anxiety attacks. I can't even put it into words — watching everybody slowly go crazy because we lost our freedom. We couldn't go anywhere without bodyguards. Back in the day, we were the type of band where we'd play a club gig and have tapes and demos we brought to hand out to people — we'd meet people, go to their house, and have keg parties and shit like that. We couldn't do that no more. We couldn't hang out with our fans. We couldn't do shit. I call it "being stuck in a box", and to this day they keep me in a fucking box — a bus, a dressing room, a hotel room, or a car. I can't be out in public. I can do it now a little more, but back then I had two fucking bodyguards, one with me twenty-four hours a day. We went k crazy during that time period. After I got sober and went through a fucking detox, after all that shit wore off, everything was good. But I remember all these emotions from that time period."

Davis said to *Metal Hammer* in December 2018; "All I remember is a lot of pain and anxiety and horrible shit. I would lie shaking in my bunk, and I'd get out onstage, and I could perform but then I'd go back to going through hell again. My therapy was that I'd hang out with my dear friend Rigger Dan. He passed away a long time ago, God bless him, but he taught me how to tie different kinds of knots, and I'd help him rig the show every night. I got involved with the crew, because everyone else was partying, and I couldn't be part of that."

Many of the tracks on *Follow The Leader* were perfect for engaging with large crowds in search of excitement. Munky said of 'Freak On A Leash' in 2018; "One of my favourite moments is the rhythmic harmonics before Jonathan does the scat boom chakas, and the build up to that drop where he says 'GO!' and kicks in the heavy groove in the middle of the song. When we wrote that together I remember thinking, 'Man, the crowd's gonna fucking lose their shit right here' and we were right."

To which Wright added; "Back then, the crowd bounce was a big thing. If that crowd wasn't bouncing, you weren't doing your job on stage."

Korn wrote songs with live audiences in mind. Upon being asked, "Do you write with the philosophy that if you can't play something in concert, you don't record it?" Silveria answered; "Yeah, we try to write like that. There are some overdubs as far as the guitar and vocals go because obviously Jonathan can't be three people at once. We try to keep it where the main parts of the songs are always possible to do live so it's not missing anything big. It's much better than bands that have one guitar player, but on the songs you hear two or three main guitar tracks. And when they play live, they pick one of the tracks to play and then it's missing a lot. It really stands out, I've always hated it when I hear bands like that."

Davis' performance style was described in *Melody Maker* in May 1999; "The tantrum is violent and unexpected. The rock star snaps suddenly and throws himself onto the floor, screaming like a spoiled kid who's been grounded for a month. He kicks his legs in the air and slams his fist into his frail body, howling louder and louder each time a punch hits home. And everyone just stands there, mouths open. His fellow band members have seen it a thousand times before, and his fans — well, they pause for a second. And then they go mental. All ten thousand of them. Jonathan Davis, Korn's kilted singer, doesn't hear a single scream, he's too far entrenched in his own private world of pain to notice the outside world. He's got a childhood of hatred, an adolescence of abuse, and an adulthood of insecurity and excess to deal with, and he has to go beyond language to articulate the rage and despair he has pent up inside. He yells, he kicks, he even breaks into a guttural gibberish that makes him sound like a caveman, and then, finally, he stands. Triumphant. Adored. And you've never experienced anything like the shouted love that young, white America offers its latest deity. An alcohol-free stadium of teenage boys and girls in sports shirts and baseball caps roars excited approval as they see all the mixed-up feelings that puberty brings acted out before them. You can sense the delight in these kids' eyes, the relief that here's a fucked-up figure who truly understands what they're going through, and they do everything they can to show their gratitude… If this were Britain, it'd be the Manics or Radiohead up there, beautiful outcasts who know what it's like to be misunderstood or alone. But this is the United States of Kick Ass America and music has to blast your brains to have any cultural resonance. So the band is Korn. And their style is the ultimate misfit hybrid: the harsh chaos of the heaviest metal, spiked with the antisocial street suss of hip-hop. And Jesus, it's popular enough to have the kids running riot and American parents up in arms."

Silveria said of Korn's on-stage chemistry; "I would say the chemistry is a very comfortable feeling. We have been playing together for so long, everyone feels like we're tight, like everyone thinking as one. Even though our backs are turned to each other on the stage, it seems like everyone is connected through the mind. Obviously there are some days that we feel like we're more "on" than other days, and we're all thinking in the same way even more."

Davis: "We just pump each other up. There's something there. We all look over at each other going off and it just pumps us up even more. We just have this chemistry together and it just works. I don't know how to explain it, it's just there."

As much as the party was in full swing, it comes across that there were times when Davis felt particularly alienated and indeed drained from the whole thing as someone who was desperately trying to kick some serious addiction habits at the time. It was reported in November 1998 under the headline of "Korn Cancel New York Show Due To Lead Singer's Exhaustion."; "Doctor's orders cancelled a scheduled Korn concert at RPI Fieldhouse in Troy, NY on Wednesday (November 4th), due to exhaustion on the part of lead singer Jonathan Davis, according to Peter Katsis of The Firm, the band's Los Angeles-based management company. 'Jonathan has reached a point of exhaustion and it was suggested by a doctor that he sit out a few days,' says Katsis. 'The doctor basically said that if we are planning on finishing the last three weeks of the tour, we'd better give him a rest.' Korn had an already scheduled day off Thursday (November 5th) and, according to Katsis, Friday's show at the Mullins Center in Amherst, Massachusetts, will go on as scheduled. The band apologised to fans in Troy and will reschedule the show at a date to be determined. The final date of the band's current tour is scheduled for November 21st in Nashville. Korn set out on the Family Values tour, which just finished up on Halloween, on September 22nd. They are scheduled to join Australia's Big Day Out tour with Marilyn Manson, among others, on January 13th in Auckland, New Zealand."

MTV News considered of the occurrence in November 1998; "Anyone who has seen the band before might not be surprised by the development given Davis' all-out on-stage antics. According to the band's management, after Korn's show in Montreal on Tuesday night, it was suggested that Davis rest for a couple of days if he expected to finish the next three weeks of the tour. 'It's nothing really serious, but it's serious enough,' the band's manager told MTV News of Davis' condition."

One of Korn's performances on the Family Values tour (Continental Airlines Arena, New Jersey, Friday 25th September) was reviewed in *Kerrang!* in October 1998; "Although Jonathan Davis barely speaks to the capacity crowds, his vocals, gestures and the music behind him do all the talking. Opening with 'It's On!', the Bakersfield crew deliver a teeth rattling set that leans heavily on material from *Follow The Leader* and sustains an intense focus and energy throughout. A hundred or so fans gyrate in the giant Korn Kage above the band, while on the floor below thousands bob up and down through 'Children Of The Korn' (during which guesting Ice Cube gets a far better reception than during his own set), 'Got The Life', 'A.D.I.D.A.S.' and a clutch of others. Korn are simply what Metallica were ten years ago — adding a fresh twist to metal, rebelling against the mainstream, and bringing an underground "fans first" sensibility to arenas. They're making the right moves. Except one. During the encore, in which the stage revolves to reveal all of Korn and Limp Bizkit as they burst into 'All In The Family', the deadliest accusation against both bands comes to mind — that some of their lyrics are homophobic and misogynist, unfortunately, a claim with considerable merit. As Durst and Davis trade "gay" slurs with each other, one wonders if this is a "family value" that these artists want to teach. Best hope not."

In many press accounts, Korn were portrayed as a group of volatile young men in search of confrontation. Fieldy was quoted in *Kerrang!* in January 1999; "You know you're doing well when people love and hate you. The funny thing is, you have to know a band to hate them. So, all you people who say you hate us probably have our records. Thanks!"

It can't have been easy though. Fieldy said in *Loudwire* in August 2019; "There were lots of times we almost broke up. We had too much of a good thing and that turned into a bad thing. We couldn't stand being around each other and we did a lot of shit just to get through the day."

Munky told *Total Guitar* in September 1998; "Bands in the past have given us all a bad reputation. I think the new generation of musicians do not behave in a stereotypical rock 'n' roll way."

This is an interesting comment because truthfully, it is now widely known that during the days of *Follow The Leader*, there was a lot of crazy stuff going on in terms of drugs and alcohol. But do addiction problems automatically mean that an artist behaves publically in a way that justifies them being given a bad reputation? It's a debate that goes beyond the scope of this book but nevertheless an interesting one. And of course, in the same feature, Munky was quoted; "I destroyed a hotel room once. I got so drunk that I really trashed the room. It was tour stress. It gets difficult. It's not an ideal situation, being on the road. But we still love it, we enjoy playing for people and it is worth enduring all the discomfort."

It was reported in *Spin* in November 1998; "Backstage, the band's five members sit in a semicircle, decked out mostly in track suits, hair piled in dreads, looking guilty of being lower-class white boys from Bakersfield, California. Over the course of the two-day festival, Korn bassist Fieldy (Reg Arvizu) will pick a fight with a member of Primal Scream by repeatedly insisting, 'You look like my uncle Bob.' An hour later, he will exasperate Garbage diva Shirley Manson by incessantly sticking a toy key chain in her face and setting off annoying sounds without a word of explanation. Meanwhile, Korn singer Jonathan Davis will yell at Goldie, 'Fuck you, dick', when the loquacious junglist doesn't recognise him, and he'll hurl insults at nice-guys Ben Folds Five every opportunity he gets. Even Junkie XL, a friendly Big Beat dance band from Amsterdam, will turn down dinner with Korn because, although they like the music, they've heard Korn are a bunch of assholes. But they're wrong. Korn aren't assholes. They just want some love, and when they don't get it they act out. 'We go to these goddamn festivals, and no fucking goddamn band will love us,' the good-naturedly angst-ridden Davis gripes in his Tokyo hotel room after a drunken night on the town. 'We get no fucking love at all. It's like we're in our own little world.

We're not that goddamn scary. What the goddamn fuck? For once in my life, please love me: I'm in Korn.'. 'We just want to be heavy,' Davis says, as if hearing the word for the first time. 'All we want to do is bring heavy back into rock 'n' roll. Because goddamned Ben Folds Five sucks. It's fucking *Cheers* music. With us, it's fucking special. We're all completely different. I'm a sissy. (Bassist) Fieldy's hip-hop, (guitarists) Head and Munky are Head and Munky, and (drummer) David's got tits' — big biceps to most people — 'but he's a great drummer. All we have in common is that we're total freaks'." (Davis' exact same dig at Ben Folds Five was also printed in *Radio & Records* in October 1998. Whether Davis was speaking in a derogatory or passionate way about music, his comment was certainly of note to the media).

The *Spin* feature continued; "Korn rank among pop's more beautifully volatile bands, a collision of egos, insecurities, and drastically different personalities. The jittery Davis is the band's nerves, the self-confident Fieldy is its brains, the 'I-got-goosebumps-watching-Björk' Munky (James Shaffer) is its heart, the obsessive-compulsive David Silveria is its muscle, and the much-smarter-than-he-pretends-to-be Head (Brian Welch) — the Angus Young-loving, Randy Rhoads-emulating teen who jump-started the band in ninth grade — is its soul. Like most successful bands, they get along like brothers; and like most brothers, they don't always get along. At one point, in the midst of privately rocking out to his band's new album, Davis hands me his headphones and cues up 'Reclaim My Place'. 'That song's about how I thought I'd become a rock star and not get picked on anymore,' he says, 'but my band still calls me a fag.' Davis pauses and reflects for a moment. 'Everyone thinks I'm queer,' he says with a sigh, 'and I kind of am — except for the dick part.' Spend any time with Davis and one is likely to be subjected to an endless barrage of queer references and gay jokes. But what might initially come across as small-town homophobia turns out to be something more, a by-product of a lifetime of sexual confusion. One Davis-penned song, entitled 'Faget', reflects on time spent as a Duran Duran-loving New Romantic, when the singer would don makeup and hang out at gay bars. 'Everyone thought I was gay my whole life,' says Davis, 'so I have to joke about it just to deal with it.' (Davis is engaged to the mother of his three-year-old son Nathan). More to the point, Davis seems to have internalised his persecutors. Those who have heard Korn only in passing may easily imagine Davis as a strapping Glenn Danzig character, screaming, growling, and raging against the world. But anyone who's spent time with the music knows that it is as much about him breaking down as it is about him fighting back."

From the same feature: "Korn's set is a disaster. The show starts late; Head cracks his noggin open on his guitar and the blackened stage is so sun-baked that the band is forced to spend much of the show with their backs to the audience, playing to actual metal fans — turned on high, they are blowing a lukewarm breeze on either side of the drummer. Though the tens of thousands of Japanese kids at the festival, never having seen Korn before, go crazy — they even open up a mosh pit (a rarity at Japanese shows) — the band is thoroughly miserable. 'We sucked,' Fieldy snaps on his way off stage. 'And you can print that.' The show takes the hardest toll on Davis, who stays up all night getting drunk in the Roppongi tourist area of Tokyo. The next day, during a group interview with the *Japan Times*, Davis suffers an anxiety attack and is rushed back to his hotel. The rest of the band covers for him, then later plunges into the exotic foreign culture, going to landmarks like the Hard Rock Cafe and Tony Roma's. Meanwhile, Davis is laid up in bed. He is watched over by Loc, the band's self-described 'doctor, psychiatrist, brother, bodyguard, and father', who was hired four years ago when Davis endured his first panic attack. Back at the hotel, Munky stands outside Davis' door. 'I feel so bad for Jonathan,' he says soft-heartedly. 'I just massaged his back. But sometimes I just don't know what to do for him.' Inside the room, Davis is smiling feebly in bed, complaining about how much the shot in his arm hurts and trying to talk Loc into blowing anal suppositories up his ass. 'My psychiatrist says he should be helping me, but he's just looking for ways to get me high,' says Davis, 'but maybe I should start taking antidepressants, or go to AA. Because when the band's joking around, the only time I feel comfortable — like I can join in — is when I'm drunk'."

Other instances in which the *Spin* feature quoted band members at their possible worst include Munky apparently having said "Manager! get me some coke! That's what managers do, isn't it?" and "Whose dick hurts from jacking off?" and Davies: "Before I got in Korn, I tried out to be Jesus Christ (Superstar) just so I could face his ass. He was such an asshole to me, but it still made me cry to watch him hang by his neck."

Perhaps there was a bit of jealousy behind some of the negative press. Fieldy was quoted in *Kerrang!* in January 1999; "When other bands meet us, we become one of their favourite bands because we're all cool as fuck and down to earth. We're like 'come on in, grab a beer.' When bands talk shit in the press, I think they're either bitter or feel threatened by us because we're out-selling them every week."

Some media accounts didn't even need to portray Korn as unpleasant people. Instead, they went straight for the music in their attack. It was advocated in *The New York Times* in September 1998; "Attitude, impact and irritation-value matter as much as music, which is why Korn has gotten away with rewriting a handful of tunes again and again. Korn has a choppy, clanky funk mode, a power-chord mode and a dissonant-riff mode; Davis tends to start out with a choked-up, haggard voice and builds up to thrash-metal growls. The character he has built up through Korn's three albums is a mess, seething with old injuries and unstable enough to cause new ones. He's wrestling with self-hatred, violent impulses, parental expectations and a confused sexual identity... Korn's songs veer from insubordination to insecurity to murderous fantasies, all in the name of what the historian Ann Douglas calls "terrible honesty", the determination to tell the whole truth no matter how brutal. Shock value makes these bands commercial and tabloid-ready. But for fans, the pain and insecurity make the music seem real."

In a more balanced account perhaps, it was observed in *Melody Maker* in May 1999: "Korn, as you will have started to gather, are not your average rock band. They play what should be the hardest noise ever — testosterone metal cut up with nasty gangsta rap beats — and yet they have a singer who's the antithesis of all that, a man who says, 'We're not machismo at all'. He's weedy, and nervy in conversation."

Davis said in *New Musical Express* in September 2019; "I hate thinking that some people hear the name Korn and think we're some douchebag, misogynistic, fucking macho dickhead band. I think the fact that we're still here says a lot."

It was asserted in *Melody Maker* in May 1999; "Jonathan's determination and honesty is what's turned Korn into a multi-million-selling act here in the US. He goes into every painful experience in his songs — family troubles in 'My Gift To You' and 'Dead Bodies Everywhere', feelings of alienation in new single 'Freak On A Leash', it goes on and on — and, like Richey Manic before him, he's become an icon for the dispossessed and the disturbed. A role he's happy to adopt."

To which Davis was quoted; "I get little kids crying and hugging me and saying, 'Thank you so much, you saved my life. It seems like I'm a hope for them. I spoke about it and it gives them a way to work the shit out. It also makes sense of my place in life, because I get to help kids out."

It is plausible that the subjects explored in Korn's songs may have informed some people's low opinion of them. The fact is though, that exploring painful feelings in their music was a strong vehicle for their creativity. Davis was quoted in *Melody Maker* in May 1999; "I was worried about losing my edge and what could I write about if I'm not depressed, but there's so much shit from going through my anxiety attacks, that this next album is going to be about that. I went fucking insane. And I'm going to write a double album based on that trip... I want to fucking make a difference. I want to be in the Rock And Roll Hall Of Fame and I want to be recognised for what I do. But I want to have fun as well. I've been through a lot and I want to reap the benefits. I may be tortured, but I still enjoy myself. I've got emotions and I put them across and I feel it, but I'm not going to let it rule my life. It ruled my life once. But now I'm happy."

Munky said to *Metal Hammer* in December 2018; "What he sang about was always dark, and even when he sings something uplifting, the band leans towards a minor key. It's just who we are. We always have a darker sound, whether it's lyrically or melodies.

I'm used to him writing that way, and none of us have ever said, 'You shouldn't say that.' As a lyricist and singer, you have to be very vulnerable and expose part of who you are, and that takes a lot of courage. He exposes a lot of fear and anxiety, and ultimately that helps people because it makes them feel less alone. He's digging so deep that nothing he pulls up cannot be gold or diamonds."

It is almost an age-old debate now as to whether or not any music categorised under the umbrella of metal has negative and aggressive intentions or at least, connotations. There was so much about Korn's image and their music that perhaps made them an easy target for bad press. Overall though, the fact is that there were multiple instances in which they reached out to their fans in ways that mattered.

Davis said of the song, 'Justin'; "Justin is a kid who's terminally ill and dying of intestinal cancer. His last dying wish was to meet us and it really freaked me out. That threw a whole bunch of new kind of pressure on my head. That's really intense. Someone's gonna die and his last thing he wants to do is come hang out with us. So I truly just freaked out. It's like, 'why would you want to meet me? What makes me so special?' And in turn, I talk about how I admire his strength and his life. I couldn't stare at him, because he was so content that he was gonna die. No one could look him in the eyes. I totally admire his strength. I wish I had it."

Davis told *Billboard* in July 1998; "We are real. We appeal to kids. There's no bullshit involved and we're doing things on our own terms."

As *Radio & Records* considered in July 2002; "Korn were perfect for a number of reasons. Musically, their eponymous 1994 debut was ground zero for the nu-metal movement and, being trend setters, they need to continue pushing the envelope. Second, Korn have always been there for their fans — not just creating legions of followers but subscribing to a lifestyle. When a Michigan student was suspended for wearing a shirt featuring the Korn logo, the band went toe to toe with the school. Through the Make A Wish Foundation, the group visited a fourteen year old fan suffering from terminal cancer (singer Jonathan Davis later wrote the song 'Justin' about the event). The band invited fans into their world via the *After School Special* — live

Internet broadcasts from the studio during the recording of *Follow The Leader*."

Davis said to *Billboard* in May 2002; "You can make music you love, but getting it out there and playing it for the kids is what gives the songs life. It's when you're out there that you see the result of your pain and work. And that's pretty damn cool. That makes it worthwhile."

It was considered in *Radio & Records* in November 1999; "Korn have such high ideals about who they are, what their music is and what it represents. That strikes a chord with a certain audience, and it develops that incredible loyalty. Those guys are originators — they're the creators. Their work is the genesis of the sound, and anybody who comes behind them has to work extra hard or find their own niche to separate them from the pack and lend themselves enough originality or generate enough passion to maintain their growth."

By 1998, Korn had a global fanbase. It is almost as if their 1998 tour schedule suggests otherwise but commercially, it was considered that it made more sense to concentrate on America following the release of their third album. Davis was quoted in *Kerrang!* in July 1998; "A lot of bands are trying to break in America. If there's an opportunity for them, they've gotta take it. America's our country, so I can understand bands wanting to be big in their country. There have been times where we've chosen not to come here (Britain) because there was a tour in the States that could really help us out. You've just got to remember to always come back."

Munky was quoted in the same feature; "It seems like British fans are way more into the music... They can do without you in America. They'll tell you 'love your shit, man' but say it really casually. British fans get more excited and they seem to know more about what's going on musically."

Fieldy said of the Family Values tour in *Kerrang!* in January 1999; "So many of the bands we liked were on it. It was such fun to watch every night. All the bands had a full production, with big stage and everything. We definitely wanna bring it over to Europe."

By several accounts, something that really went against Korn in terms of their reputation was Woodstock '99. Whilst the very name of Woodstock carried connotations of love, peace and kindness, Woodstock '99 was a very different affair altogether, with a number of attendees reporting incidents of sexual assault and drug overdoses. Eventually, tensions culminated into riots and fires during sets from Limp Bizkit and the Red Hot Chili Peppers. The chaos expanded as vendor trucks were ransacked, most things of value were looted and portable toilets were shoved over or destroyed, spreading more human waste on the ground than there was already.

On balance, it is considered by some that poor organisation played a large part in what happened at Woodstock '99. Initially, poor sanitation and overpriced food and drink had already affected the morale of the festival goers. In a series of frustrations that led up to the fire, an anti-gun group passed candles around that were intended to be lit during the Red Hot Chili Peppers' performance of 'Under The Bridge'. The candles however, proved to be perfect ammunition for anyone who wanted to set fire to the mounds of rubbish that had already built up throughout the festival. Ironically, the Chili Peppers played a cover of Jimi Hendrix's 'Fire' that day.

Uncomfortable statistics attributed to Woodstock '99 includes forty-four arrests as well as ten thousand people who required medical intervention. The fact that the reported rapes took place in mosh pits with multiple aggressors, all as the bands performed, left everyone who set foot onto the festival with something of a black mark against their name, purely by association! Limp Bizkit and Korn were given a particularly bad name for what happened but on balance, the assaults were not committed exclusively during any one particular act. This is an important point considering that there were also female friendly acts who performed at Woodstock '99, including Alanis Morissette.

Bearing in mind that Korn played on the first day of the festival, Davis said in *The Ringer* in August 2018; "Dude, our day went perfect. Korn had the best show, we fucking killed that shit. It was the second day when all that shit happened, when Limp Bizkit went on and told them to "break stuff". Of course, they were just being punk rock — you didn't need to take that literally and fucking tear the place down. They got blamed for that shit, but (the festival organisers) were selling a bottle of water for ten bucks. You had to walk around in piss, because no one was there dumping the fucking porta-potties. So piss and shit was everywhere. You get that many people in an area and that shit goes on, people are gonna get in a bad mood, so it was just natural for that shit to happen."

John Scher, president of Metropolitan Entertainment Group, one of Woodstock 99's producers, was quoted in *Billboard* in June 2000; "Obviously we've got some problems with this generation of concertgoers not having appropriate respect for each other. In regard to that, Woodstock wasn't an isolated incident, it was just bigger."

In the same feature, Ken Viola, director of security for Metropolitan was quoted, "In some ways I believe the kids were trying to make a point about their frustration and anger, and they made that point. Unfortunately, that point doesn't bode well for any more mass gatherings of that nature... At Woodstock '99, the majority of the music was geared towards that new element, which I call the Blank Generation — they seem to be more anger oriented and the music is designed as a way for individuals to release anger and frustration."

The article went as far as stating that "hard rock fans of bands like Limp Bizkit, Korn, Rage Against The Machine, and Metallica are among the rowdiest." Charming! Everyone who's reading this book had better slam it down right away and get back to all of that rioting and destruction that you're apparently into!

Overall, it wasn't Woodstock '99 that signified the end of Korn's commercial heyday. The rise of Internet piracy had begun to play a large part in how music was in a suddenly vulnerable position. Not only did it impact record sales in a large way but it also changed the extent to which record companies had to keep ahead of the game and sometimes, this would hit a band financially. Certainly, a sign of the times but very much one that Korn were part of.

Chapter Four
A Legendary Album

From their very first album in 1994, Korn's music was innovative, fresh and worthy of attention. There was no other band that sounded like Korn when they first came onto the scene with their debut. The release of *Follow The Leader* in 1998 took the band to new commercial heights. Not only that though; it played a large part in introducing Korn's sound into the mainstream, as well as the genre of nu-metal in general.

Follow The Leader, and indeed singles from the album, 'Got The Life' and 'Freak On A Leash', made Korn a household name and increased their cult following. This was quite the achievement at a time when the charts were dominated by the likes of Britney Spears, Backstreet Boys and the Spice Girls. Davis told *The Fader* in August 2018; "It was the *Total Request Live* age — boy bands and pop stars — and we were just flying the torch at that time for rock music."

Whilst *Follow The Leader* made a big impact on rock music, the range of genres embraced on the album is such that its long term influence goes beyond just rock music. Munky told *Metal Hammer* in December 2018; "There's also a lot of hip-hop guys who got into that album, fifteen or twenty years younger than me, and that stuff influenced a lot of urban kids, which is cool, and it's tricky keeping people's attention and keeping them as fans, but we had hardcore fans from the first records and *Follow The Leader* blew us up. I'm floored by it."

Korn's albums prior to *Follow The Leader* — *Korn* and *Life Is Peachy* — were still important contributors in Korn's journey to success. It was considered in *Spin* in May 1998; "Listening to Korn is like trying to figure out what you love about a rollercoaster ride: the ordered climb or the chaotic freefall; the fear of impending danger or the release of fear itself. 'We blew the door open for heavy music in 1994,' says confident vocalist Jonathan Davis. 'And our new album is even heavier. Dancier. There's a deeper groove. We've taken advantage of technology.' Threat or promise, metal experimentalists Korn have spent the past four years readying for their inevitable breakthrough: two platinum records, a Grammy nomination, a headlining spot on last year's Lollapalooza tour, and their own record label (Elementree) on which they will be "pimping" out some "bad-ass shit". Not since Rage Against The Machine declared 'Fuck you/I won't do what you tell me' has a band issued anthemic ultimatums and received such undying devotion in return, generating the kind of loyalty that would make the Heaven's Gate guy jealous. So it's with equal parts ambition and bravado that the Bakersfield, California, natives are planning this fall's Family Values tour, an arena extravaganza of Lilithian proportions complete with break dancing crews, fire eaters, and likeminded musical brutes Orgy and Limp Bizkit. 'Palooza was pretty fucking stale,' says Davis. 'We wanted to do a festival of up-and-coming harder-edge bands, because we don't get a chance to be heard, really.' While Korn may be a household name among the aggro set, they've been virtually ignored by the mainstream press, radio, and MTV. Look for the children of the Korn to enjoy the last laugh."

It was advocated in *Radio & Records* in October 2003; "In 1994 Korn sprouted from the underground with their self-titled debut. While it built slowly, *Korn* was the sound of a new movement. Just throw the disc back into your player, and you'll hear the moment a newer, more violent breed of hard rock came rolling down the mountain. Quiet cymbals, watery guitars, deeper-than-a-mineshaft bass and a mortuary scientist-turned-singer Jonathan Davis growling 'Are you ready?' just before the whole damn thing collapses into an anguished torrent of downtuned seven-string Ibanezes. Richter-scale beats and brain shaking bass. This was 'Blind' and it opened the eyes and ears of a new generation of rock fans. For better or worse, the group spawned a whole new sound and a host of imitators... With 1996's *Life Is Peachy*, they gained even more steam and broke through to platinum sales before 1998's *Follow The Leader* finally established the group at radio with hits like 'Got The Life' and 'Freak On A Leash'."

Upon being asked how *Follow The Leader* compared to Korn's last two albums, Davis said to *Kerrang!* in July 1998; "We've taken the best elements of both albums and turned 'em into something really neat. Sonically, it's way better."

Munky added; "In some parts it's heavier, in other parts it's more hip-hoppy. We took a look at the first two records before starting out. The first had a groundbreaking sound. The grooves are real good on the second, but we didn't give 'em enough time to develop."

****

The success of *Follow The Leader* presented Korn with a whole host of new opportunities. It was advocated in *Spin* in November 1998; "Korn's previous album, 1996's *Life Is Peachy*, entered the Billboard pop charts at number three. Today, Korn has its own label, Elementree; its own arena festival, the Family Values tour, with Limp Bizkit, Ice Cube, Rammstein, and Orgy; and, the most impressive fuck-you to the gatekeepers of pop-taste who have shown them no love, their own number one album, *Follow The Leader*, which topped the Billboard pop charts in its first week, selling 268,000 copies. This means that Korn are no longer an underground phenomenon, playing heavy, low-end, hip-hop-conscious, Gothic-leaning thrash-rock for skate-kids and misfits so intensely b(r)and loyal that they stopped wearing Stussy and started wearing Adidas in emulation of their antiheroes (who, thanks to a new sponsorship, now wear custom-designed Puma). Korn is now officially part of the major leagues — members of an elite cadre of rock bands that have had number one albums this decade, bands like the Smashing Pumpkins, Dave Matthews, R.E.M., and Skid Row."

As the album's title implies, *Follow The Leader* was intended as something of a middle finger salute to other bands who were trying to copy Korn's sound. Munky said to *Metal Hammer* in December 2018; "Now we think it's cool, but at the time we were like, 'Man, this is bullshit, people trying to sound like Korn.' We'd created something that was different, but right after the *Life Is Peachy* album we were starting to hear bands that sounded like us, so we took a left turn. They thought they knew the formula, and all of a sudden we put out this record that's hip-hop, rock, metal. If you listen to the first album and *Follow The Leader*, it's almost like two different bands."

Over twenty years later and the impact of *Follow The Leader* is certainly not one to be overlooked. It is considered by some to be a strong contender in having brought the genre of nu-metal into the mainstream to an extent that many other bands were keen to follow in Korn's footsteps by creating the same sound right into the new millennium and beyond. Whilst Davis himself has often advocated against the term nu-metal, there is still a lot to be said for what Korn's album did for rock and metal, no matter how you fine tune the categories. He was quoted of the term "nu-metal" in *The Ringer* in August 2018; "That was something they fucking came up with to lump us in with what we started. All the bands that followed, *those* are nu-metal bands. You don't call fucking Metallica some thrash band. They helped fucking usher in that kind of music."

Whether or not Davis himself was happy to have Korn, their brand and their music categorised under the umbrella of nu-metal, the fact is that the fusion of musical styles that Korn embraced on *Follow The Leader* offered an exciting example of what was possible when heavy baselines, distorted guitar, agonised vocals and rap were combined.

Davis said in *Loudwire* in August 2019; "We were listening to tons of rap, but we also liked bands like Pantera and Sepultura and as we evolved, I think we learned to mix those two styles better. Plus, I grew up on new wave and I always wanted to make music that had lots of melody. We got that into the first two records, but *Follow The Leader* was where we were able to really emphasise the hooks and people loved that shit... We never wanted to sound like every other band. Even though we liked all those bands that were part of the sound that we helped create, we've always wanted to be one step ahead of everyone else who was doing this kind of music."

Munky told *Guitarist* in October 1998; "The album is more mature and it has more of a hip-hop vibe. Some people have said it's heavier, others have said it's less extreme, but whatever! I'm just really pleased with the response so far."

Korn's rise to fame in the mainstream was a double-edged sword in terms of the experiences it afforded them. On the one hand it raised their profile as musicians (so much so that they are still going strong today) but equally, it presented new pressures for them as human beings who were already facing a range of demons. As Davis' addiction became a growing concern, he made the decision that he needed to stop. He said in *The Fader* in August 2018; "In the end, it was necessary. It had to happen for me to realise what a fucking out of control motherfucker I was, because it made me become sober — which, in turn, saved my life and my band, because my bandmates were ready to fucking kill me."

In *Kerrang!* in May 2018 he said; "I got sober really quick. I was sober at twenty-eight years old. In August it'll be twenty fucking years since I had a drink. I had to stop because I was drinking a gallon of Jack Daniel's or a litre of Jäger a night — I was out of my fucking mind. Two things made me stop: firstly, my band started to hate me; and secondly, I had a son. I would come home drunk and my son would see that shit. I stay sober for my three boys now, because I want to be an example to them. I don't want them to see me being a fucked-up dumbass. I switched the addiction out for music. When everyone else would be going out and partying, I'd be on the bus, writing on my laptop."

In deciding to go sober whilst being committed to the Korn Kampaign and then the Family Values tour, Davis certainly had a lot on his plate. As phenomenal as the commercial success and musical impact of *Follow The Leader* was, the fact is that such achievement was tainted with difficulty on a personal level. Being sober presented Davis with exacerbated anxiety struggles, so much so that there were times where he had to be put on suicide watch. Even with all the success in the world, that can't be a good experience.

Whilst Davis' personal struggles of 1998 are well documented, he wasn't alone in them. Fieldy said in *Kerrang!* in January 1999; "I had different issues, but I can relate to where Jonathan is coming from. Sometimes on tour, late at night, we'll sit up and totally vent stuff for five hours. In the morning we'll feel a lot better... It's just when a lot of Korn stuff is going on that it gets overwhelming. Sometimes the best thing to do is go somewhere in a room by yourself. I'll go and sit in the back of the bus for an hour and just look at the wall. Jon likes people to be around him when he's having anxiety, but I can't even have people touch me."

Munky told *The Fader* in August 2018; "Jonathan got sober a lot quicker than the rest of us did, so he saw things that the rest of us wish we had seen earlier. He saw a lot of the dirty, shady music-business components earlier than we recognised because we were too busy getting hammered."

In *Metal Hammer* in December 2018 Munky said; "It was good in the sense that we were able to buy new cars and upgrade from apartments to condos, but it was also bad to give five guys money — we were all addicts, just buying alcohol and not thinking about tomorrow or our future. I didn't really deal with it very well. The money was new to us — we didn't grow up with money — so it wasn't like we had some financial advisor sitting us down and going, 'You need to put money away.' None of us had any of that until a few years ago, which is kinda sad. It was tough; you have all this money and a lot of addiction problems, and you buy dumb shit when you're fucked up! Cars and boats, there's no appreciation. And all of a sudden you have this crew of ten people, all these guys who wanna leach off you and pretend that they're helping you. But the only person that's gonna help you is your mom. Everybody else is out to fucking take your money and it took me a while to see that."

Head spoke of the impact the success had on him in *Metal Hammer* in December 2018; "The friends I grew up with, and the guy I looked in the mirror at, they all became different people. I just couldn't control the habits. I wanted to drink alcohol and have fun, and maybe do drugs once in a while, but I didn't want them to rule me. Also, my personality — I was good with the guys and I could have fun, but in relationships I was insecure and I never felt good enough. When the fame came, it just magnified all those insecurities."

In 2005 and with a methamphetamine addiction, Head left Korn for a period of eight years, during which he became a born-again

Christian. He said to *Loudwire* in September 2019; "Everyone has a great outlook on life right now. We got past all that stupid drug addiction and rockstar mentality — all that stuff's gone."

He told *The Ringer* in August 2018; "I didn't want to become this person that people don't like. I wanted to show people that I was kind. My parents are just really kind and nice people, and I think that was instilled into me."

Perhaps it really is lonely at the top. 1998 was hard work for Korn and that remained the case as they went into 1999. Fieldy said in *Kerrang!* in January 1999; "It's been a long road, man. We've worked our asses off! After doing Family Values, we jumped right on to another Korn headlining tour. Altogether, it was nine weeks. Towards the end we started losing our minds a little bit. Once you get onstage you forget about everything, but that's only an hour of the day. The rest of the time we're hanging around together — and just like any roommates, you get a little irritated with each other. Luckily, we're more like brothers, so when we do get in an argument, the next day we're like 'hey, how's it going?'… We had a couple of little arguments. Being "rock stars", we almost forgot that we're actually roommates. You have to treat each other accordingly sometimes. Take a step back."

Despite the personal difficulties affecting Korn at the time, the Family Values tour was important to their career, and indeed that of other artists. Davis said in *Metal Hammer* in March 2018; "This idea started super early. For years, we always wanted to do a festival and put something together that was new. We went back and forth with our management and figured out what we were going for and how to do it. It was fun to do. It was about showing what was going on at that time. We were at a turning point in heavy music and it felt huge and we wanted to put something on that showed what the fuck was going on. Everyone was given a full production so it felt like you were getting a headline show from all of the bands: Limp Bizkit with their big-ass spaceship, and we had the Korn Kage that put kids on the stage, rocking out with us. I think the cage was Fieldy's idea and to this day, I still think it's one of the coolest things we've ever done. It served its purpose in the way it exposed people to what was going on at that time and what we were doing in Korn. It blew everything up. It was the first time we ever played arenas and it seemed everyone who was on that tour — except for Cube, who was already huge — blew up and were playing bigger shows after. It was a steppingstone to all of our bands and that scene taking over for a couple of years... We were convinced we needed to have a hip-hop act on there. We all listened to hip-hop at that time and it was a big influence on us and the scene, and who better than Ice Cube? That was the shit. It was awesome. That guy is a legend and people had to respect that. I didn't worry about the crowd not taking to him at all because he ripped it up every night and you can't deny that. He was bringing old N.W.A. into his set and the crowd loved it. The kids who liked us and Bizkit came from the same school of thought as us so having Cube on there made total sense to everyone. We always tried to get Deftones on the tour but we could never figure it out. Other than that, it was the exact bill that we wanted to put on the road. Everyone hung out and it was a good time, but it was when I was dealing with anxiety for the first time so I spent a lot of time in my bunk. I remember everyone in the band had a great time and got along with every other band and there was no bitching — it was an amazing tour."

Like all artistic products, they are very much of their time; they are reflective of where the creators behind the magic were at with things during that point in their lives. Whilst such product can become iconic, it is simply a snapshot in time. *Follow The Leader* is no different. Korn were young men finding their way both personally and professionally at the time.

Davis recalled in *The Ringer* in August 2018; "I used the movie *The Doors* with Val Kilmer as my textbook in rock 'n' roll school to be a rock star. I thought I had to be what that was — being all fucked up, doing drugs and getting drunk, fucking as many fucking chicks as I could, the whole nine."

In *Melody Maker* in May 1999 he said: "You see Mötley Crüe and all this debauchery and alcohol and drugs and think, 'That's what I have to do to be a rock star.' So I started drinking a bottle of Jack and a bottle of Jägermeister a day. I'd wake up at three (in the afternoon, obviously), go to the studio, crack open the fucking Jack and call it Jack O'clock. I'd drink thirty Jack and Cokes every night. And then my mental problems started. I fucking went crazy. I was fucking schizo... I was a fucking upper kid. I loved speed, I loved cocaine, and I loved booze. And I'd be spun out, sleep-deprived and hearing shit. I was a speed freak for two years. You're up for three days, go down for a day, and you have to do lines to get out of bed again."

Munky spoke of the days of making *Follow The Leader* with great fondness in an interview on KLOS 95.5 with DJ Full Metal Jackie in June 2018; "Because we were really young, and it really was the first bit of money that we started to see from so many years of hard work. And we just really had a lot of fun. And musically, we experimented with collaborations. We were in a real studio, in North Hollywood, in the middle of town. Because we recorded our first two records with (producer) Ross Robinson up at Indigo Ranch, and that was so remote and removed from anything, and that's how he liked it. But once we had the freedom and the money and the record label support to get into a real studio and have, like, a real beer budget. I think, honestly, the making of that album was something like thirty thousand dollars in alcohol by the time it was all done."

People change. Davis said in *Metal Hammer* in January 2019; "Korn lived the rock 'n' roll lifestyle to the fullest. It was so much fun that I can't hardly remember most of it. It was the most amazing time. We were notorious for that shit. It's nice to look back on it now and say it was fun but I wouldn't go down that road again. We're all sober and that helps a lot. We're all a little bit grown up now, so we don't fight over stupid shit. We've all got families and we're watching our kids grow up. It's pretty crazy." Upon being asked, "If you had the chance to do it all over again, would you do anything differently?", Davis said; "Nothing. It all led to something that led to something that led to something that got me here, so I wouldn't change a fucking thing."

****

With Korn's third album being so of its time, there are some elements of it that are a source of embarrassment for them today. They have been candid about this publically. Probably one of the most controversial tracks on the album, 'All In The Family' is abundant in homophobic slurs. It hasn't featured on Korn's live setlist for years to this point. Whilst the song might have felt like a good idea in 1998, it hasn't stood the test of time. The *Los Angeles Times* argued in December 2003 that it was "a duet of cheap insults with Bizkit's Fred Durst that only diminishes one of Korn's strongest albums."

In the same vein, in August 1998 the *Winston-Salem Journal* asserted that "one wonders how Davis could stumble so badly with 'All In The Family' — a scatological song crammed with crude jive and anti-gay jibes that severely undercuts an otherwise potent disc."

The *Austin-American Statesman* considered that the song's "pulsating rhythms are undermined by countless references to guys' private parts, the f word, "faggots" and incest."

On balance though, in August 1998, The *Los Angeles Times* attempted to comprehend what Korn's intention might have been in making a song so full of uncomfortable slurs; "The homophobic epithets, the band might say, were not meant to disparage gays, but rather meaningless, street-talking jive by two guys "playing the dozens", greatly influential on rap — of verbal combat that emphasises the competitive trading of fanciful insults. After all, the title 'All In The Family' calls back that lovable TV bigot, Archie Bunker, doesn't it?... The ugliness of 'All In The Family' doesn't stem from overt homophobia; let's take Davis at his word that he harbours no ill feelings toward gays. Instead, it embodies the ingrained, unthinking homophobic bias that runs strong in our culture."

Davis told *The Ringer* in August 2018; "We were fucking out of our minds, insanely drunk and high when we did that. It's like that scene out of *Boogie Nights*, when they were all fuckin' on crack and they're like, 'No no, this is the best shit ever!'"

In the same regard, Davis has also dismissed the song, 'Cameltosis' in recent years, stating that as with 'All In The Family', it was also a juvenile exercise. He was quoted in *The Ringer* in August 2018; "What the fuck was I fucking thinking? I was twenty-seven. I was still really immature."

He said of 'Cameltosis' in *New Musical Express* in September 1998; "I'm not saying all women are bitches and cunts. I'm saying, fuck all bitches and cunts."

To which Fieldy was quoted, "You can tell we're not women bashing."

The interviewer then asserted that surely the average young male rock fan might take the song as being entirely anti women. Davis' response: "Well that's his problem. When I write I don't expect to be responsible for what our fans do. It's not my problem if they're fucked up in the head."

The interviewer made a good point, or at least touched upon, the concept that perhaps musicians have a social responsibility to not put stuff out there that could be a damaging influence to young music fans but equally, as Davis was getting at, why should any artist be responsible for how any other individual perceives something?

In 2018, for the twentieth anniversary of *Follow The Leader*, it was initially assumed that Korn would perform the full album live at a small handful of US tour dates — September 12th at the Masonic in San Francisco, September 13th at the Palladium in Los Angeles, and September 15th at the Pearl Theatre in Las Vegas. However, as Munky explained to KLOS 95.5 DJ Full Metal Jackie in June 2018, "There's some songs that we did collaborations — we (had guest appearances by) Tre (Trevant Hardson) from The Pharcyde, which is a hip-hop group; Ice Cube — everybody knows Ice Cube; and Fred (Durst) from Limp Bizkit. So those are the songs that are, like, 'Okay, well, we can't really recreate that.' But we're gonna play a handful of the songs that people haven't heard and maybe we haven't played in twenty years." Just as well really considering tracks like 'Cameltosis' and 'All In The Family'.

As much as *Follow The Leader* and all that came with it documents a turbulent time for Korn in terms of some personal issues, there were also some fantastically positive things to come out of the album's success. Head considered that the album was a major catalyst in the turning point of when his father began to respect him. He said to *The Ringer* in August 2018; "My dad and I butted heads a little bit, because of the long hair and the makeup. He was just more traditional. He became so proud of me. How many musicians actually make it? It was a cool time, man."

When *Follow The Leader* was at its commercial peak, Korn were everywhere, from MTV to patches on the backpacks and clothes of young people who could relate to the angst communicated in Davis' lyrics. It could be considered that Korn's third album had a significant impact on youth culture at the time. It is understandable really, considering the way in which they used the Internet, music television and promotional touring as the powerful marketing tool that it was at the time.

In an interview on KLOS 95.5 with DJ Full Metal Jackie in June 2018, Munky stated that *Follow The Leader* represented "a really special moment" in Korn's career: "That's when MTV was hitting, and everybody was watching all these boy bands. And then Korn topping the charts of all the *Total Request Live* stuff. I feel like it was a turning point. I feel like if you didn't like the whole boy band thing and the pop thing, you had us over here."

It was considered in *Spin* in November 1998; "Writing and performing such intensely personal songs has never been much of a problem for Korn; reaching a mass audience, however, has been a different story. Ignored by the mainstream press, radio, and MTV, the group over the years has cultivated its loyal fan base by touring relentlessly, creating a much talked-about website and weekly Internet *After School Special* (Korn TV), and devising stunts like crossing the country on a mock political campaign via private plane to promote the new album (it worked: MTV's John Norris dispatched regular reports from the jet). In the process, Korn has spawned its own mini-scene, with bands like the Deftones, Limp Bizkit, and Coal Chamber following in Korn's post-metal footsteps, not to mention the scores of dirty dreadlocked imitators that have cropped up in Bakersfield."

Al Masocco, VP of marketing at Epic Records, was quoted in the same feature; "The cool thing about Korn is that they take more fans in at the top but don't lose any at the bottom. That's the design of the band — they're built for the road. They're street tough."

Upon being asked how he would like Korn to be remembered, Davis said in 1998; "For starting a new kind of music, a new scene.

Like fucking Led Zeppelin or something! Ultimately, what we wanna do is become as big as possible."

To which Munky was quoted, "While still remaining respected as musicians. We won't be coming out with some radio hit song and losing our fanbase."

The fact that in 1998, the Internet was still in its prime and still not a strong presence in many households meant that for Korn, things were going just right in that regard; whilst the Internet was available and an excellent vehicle for broadcasting to fans from the recording studio, this was still during the days that steaming music online wasn't a norm.

Head said in 2018; "It's really cool to be able to say that we were involved in the mainstream MTV before all things changed. That excitement waiting to see your favourite band's video on TV back then — that's just not happening anymore. As soon as someone puts a video out, you just watch it over and over. That excitement of not being able to have it when you wanted it was something special."

Even by more modern standards, 'Got The Life' and 'Freak On A Leash' wouldn't sound out of place at a house party today; both songs contain memorable hooks and structurally aren't too different from a typical pop song, at least, in the majority of parts anyway.

Fieldy said of 'Freak On A Leash' in 2018; "When we did that song, we definitely knew this was going to be one of the hits. I wish I had a better word for that — I know people hate that word, because it's not like we were trying to make some pop hit or something. One of the classics. It stands out. What really took it over the top was when the middle part broke down, and then Jonathan came in and started doing that weird, almost-reggae beatboxing crazy scat voice. That almost made the whole song, what everybody waits for. Right when that hit, we just knew that song was special."

Davis said; "Everybody made a bajillion memes about the 'mmbop da mmbob da nena.' That's just purely heavy scatting, I just felt like some percussive shit. I did that on *Life Is Peachy* when I did 'Twist', that was really the heavy scat. I was beatboxing because I love to beatbox... That comes from Doug E. Fresh and shit like that, old school hip-hop. Doug E. Fresh was the best beatboxer back then."

Fieldy said; "Jonathan was a DJ, then a drummer, then a singer. That's how he has that rhythmic vocal going on. I couldn't even karaoke that — I wouldn't know what to do." Munky: "I remember saying, 'Wow, that sounds like a rap sort of track.' Everybody got excited because it sounded so different from the previous albums."

With the success of *Follow The Leader* being what it was, it is easy to forget that it was very much new territory for Korn. Fieldy said; "It was different back then because it was all not really knowing what we were doing. You can hear it in the way the song turned out. If you hear the songs we do today, you can hear that we know what we're doing a little more. But I think that's why people like 'Freak On A Leash' — because it's kind of raw."

It's a little ironic perhaps on the basis that throughout their rise to higher levels of stardom, Korn were adamant that if their music happened to have mainstream appeal, it was more of a coincidence than due to a deliberate move on their part. In the long run though, the mainstream success has certainly not been cause for complaint. Upon being asked whether he was concerned that Korn's mainstream success had tainted their image of being "a band of outcasts", Davis was quoted in *Kerrang!* in May 2018; "Inside I was smiling, thinking, 'Look at me, motherfucker!' How could I not? It was the best revenge ever. All those people that used to call me a faggot and all that shit when I was in school could go eat a great big fucking dick. I didn't want to hurt anybody, but I wanted to flaunt my shit in front of them to say 'fuck you!' All those tough guys ended up being loser fucks, while the people they called faggots ended up being successful."

Time can be a great healer. Upon being asked "In old Korn interviews, around the time of the first album, maybe even more so the second, you talk about the massive success you achieved being a 'fuck you' to those who doubted you, people who bullied you, people who did bad things to you. Do you still feel like that now?", Davis told *New Musical Express* in September 2019; "Oh no. I don't give a flying fuck what people like that think now! The difference is that I'm a forty-eight-year-old man now, and I was twenty-four when I said that stuff. What did I know, really? I do not give a single bit of energy to anyone I would have been bothered about back then. But back then it really, really mattered to me. Everything we achieved felt like a 'fuck you' to people who'd done us wrong. Time helps introduce wisdom to you. My advice? Let that shit go... I think the thing with Korn, is we've always done what we've wanted to and never followed anyone else. I think we'll work out a way to make sense going forward. We're survivors. We transcend."

In 2007, a new generation of fans were introduced to 'Freak On A Leash' when Davis performed it as a duet with Amy Lee from Evanescence for MTV *Unplugged* (it had been recorded at MTV studios at Times Square in New York City on December 9th 2006). The song was adapted in a way that offered a new texture to it whereby Lee added melodic vocalisations in place of where Davis beatboxed on the original version of the song. In 2015, President Obama advocated positively of Korn. Time and time again, *Follow The Leader* and indeed Korn themselves are never far removed from reference.

Whilst the sentiment behind 'Freak On A Leash' was anti music industry, over time, it was a key catalyst in solidifying Korn's career. Davis said; "That's what that song is about — I just felt like everyone was using and abusing me. Then that record just made it ten times worse. That's how it goes, but it's all good. Looking back, I think it's amazing I get to do what I love for a living. It's not work."

Head said; "I'm really proud of that record, most of the songs, and what we accomplished. Bringing those unique songs to the genre of heavy rock and metal helped set our career up — and we still have a career." 'Got The Life' and 'Freak On A Leash' are classic Korn songs to this day and were featured on the setlist for their winter tour in 2020.

The power of hindsight. Fieldy said; "I don't think I would change anything — I'm pretty happy with it. There's probably a hundred different things that we did where I wish we wouldn't have done this and that — tell you the truth, I like it. It's classic. That's one of them where I'm alright, even when we play it, every part flows, every part feels good. Most singles, bands do hate. There's a lot of our singles that I do hate playing, I'm not gonna say which ones. This happened to be one that's pretty solid, and I'm thankful."

It is plausible that, as eccentric as some of the tracks are on *Follow The Leader*, songs from the album that were released as singles still hold up well today. 'Freak On A Leash', for instance, as heavy as it is, is melodic and memorable. Fieldy said; "I remember going, are we getting punk'd? It doesn't make sense. Everything flew so fast, I was still in denial about a lot of it. Looking back now, maybe it stood out so far that people took a liking to it. It was just odd enough, but not too far off."

Toby Wright added; "It was the melody, the heaviness of it. We knew we made the soundscape strange but still very catchy. There were a lot of guitar and vocal hooks. We loaded that one down with those hooks... Jonathan made it that much better by really singing his butt off on that song."

In November 1999, just fifteen months after the release of *Follow The Leader*, Korn released their next album, *Issues*. With the new millennium on the horizon, Korn were still a big name. Whilst *Issues* didn't make the commercial impact that *Follow The Leader* did, it still did well enough that thereafter, Korn next began working on one of their more ambitious albums, *Untouchables*. It is considered by some that the album was a casualty of the time in which it was released; by 2002 the rise of the Internet increased the possibilities of music piracy and it was a difficult time for the music industry overall. It was considered in *Radio & Records* in October 2003; "In 1999 *Issues* brought more platinum and more raves, but while 2002's *Untouchables* sold more than 1.3 million copies, it was viewed by many as a misstep."

Despite *Untouchables* not reaching the commercial heights that *Follow The Leader* did, sonically, it is a fascinating album. It is experimental and broad ranging in how Korn explored greater possibilities on their overall sound at the time. Davis was quoted in *The Independent* in May 2017; "*Untouchables* is still my favourite Korn record."

Whilst the album cost four million dollars to make at the time, it was a worthwhile endeavour. Davis told *The Independent* in May 2017; "The record I'm most proud of is *Untouchables*... The production on it is of the same calibre in terms of sonic quality. We spent a lot of money making that record and it took us two years to make; I remember we spent a month just getting drum sounds. (Michael) Beinhorn is my favourite producer ever, he's just got a great ear and he's not afraid to tell you if you suck. I'd do vocal takes and think they were the best and then he'd tell me to go home because he thought my voice wasn't right. I'd get so mad at him, but I love him. It was so much work; if I can find the footage, I'm going to put a little documentary together about that record because it's a one of a kind that will never be made again."

Innovatively, *Untouchables* was recorded in 96kHz and fifty mics were set up to record just one drum kit. A lot of time and care went into making the album, so much so that Davis spent six months working on the vocals (this was largely due to the multi-tracking). He said in 2018; "I know tons of soundmen who use that record to check their P.A.s"

By the early new millennium, whilst Korn were no longer a big deal in the mainstream, their music was certainly still commercially viable and was supported by a core fan base, many of whom had followed the band since the release of their debut album in 1994. However, with Internet hitting record sales across the music industry, when Korn came to doing their next album in 2003 — *Take A Look In The Mirror* — they had to be a lot more budget conscious whereby songs were written on the road and they produced the album themselves.

How ironic that the Internet, the very thing that helped them market *Follow The Leader* in 1998, was later in some ways, the enemy! On balance though, as it stands, the record industry favours some genres more than others. Whilst the genre of choice is an ever-changing variable, it is certainly something that has informed how things turned out for Korn. Davis said in 2018; "Epic really spent a lot of fucking money on us and believed in us, and we wouldn't have got where we got if they wouldn't have pushed and done what they did. At this time, the labels don't have money like that. I mean, they don't for rock. They do it for hip-hop now and pop music. I think we were the last guard."

Artistically though, it could be argued that *Take A Look In The Mirror* didn't suffer on account of the context in which it was made. Davis told *The Independent* in May 2017; "We had a mobile studio set-up out on the road with us so we'd fuck around and come up with riffs. We wanted to do something that was stripped down and raw, so we just wrote some songs out on the road and put it together and made a record."

It was reported in *Billboard* in December 2005; "*Take A Look In The Mirror* and *Untouchables* were leaked to the Internet prior to their street (release) dates."

With Head having left the band in 2005 in 2006, so did Silveria. On balance though, how many bands manage to maintain a line-up for over a decade? That's pretty impressive on Korn's part, comparatively speaking.

The innovative use of technology on *Follow The Leader* was such that Korn have continued to use similar approaches to making their music from that point onwards. Munky said; "A lot of that stuff we still use now — the DigiTech and Whammy pedals — to get that DJ-sounding element in the guitar sounds. We play a lower-tuned seven-string guitar, so with the Whammy pedal it was like, 'Whoa, we can make the low end go even lower and the high end go up to fucking dog-ear shit'."

Toby Wright still holds *Follow The Leader* in high regard; "*Follow The Leader* is right up there with Metallica's ...*And Justice For All*, with some Alice In Chains records. I worked my tail off on this record. I loved working on it — it was one of those records where you keep on keeping on no matter how difficult it got, because I believed in it so much."

For many fans *Follow The Leader* still feels incredibly relevant and ranks high on their frame of reference. For Korn though, as the people who were there and actually made it happen, it perhaps feels like something that is very much behind them. Davis said in *New Musical Express* in September 2019; "I've always considered making music my therapy so what I tried to do was flood my life with music… What music does — what it's always done — is give me a place to put the shit that's in my head, that stops me from just exploding. All the shit that has happened to me is in Korn records. Each one is like a time capsule of shit. I don't like listening back to them because that's painful, but getting it out of my head, onto the page — I write lyrics like I'm in a stream of consciousness — then into the music — that's kept me going."

The joys of spontaneity and stream of consciousness writing. Davis told *The Guardian* in October 2016; "I'll sit there with a pen and paper and I'll start writing. Sometimes, I have no clue what the fuck I'm talking about."

Davis was quoted of *Follow The Leader*'s twentieth anniversary in 2018; "Holy fuck, I can't believe it's twenty years. In all honesty, that's some shit in the past."

Fair point really, considering that today, Korn are — as they always have been — ever-keen to move forward with their music. He was quoted in *Vice* in September 2019; "If you make the same record over and over again, then you become like a nostalgic act. You have to roll with the times and just keep stuff fresh and new to stay relevant."

Not of course, that wanting to move forward with new ideas is to negate what has already been achieved. In *Kerrang!* in May 2018, Davis asserted; "I'm happy with the body of work I've been responsible for... I never wanted to conform or do the same thing over and over. I wanted to push the envelope."

One of the most fascinating things about music is that it never stands still. There is always something new and what could be successfully marketed to a previous generation's youth would possibly stand out like a sore thumb by today's standards. Endearingly perhaps, *Follow The Leader* may be no different. Davis said in 2018; "I think critics, mostly the older ones, it just went over their heads. If I tried to fucking write shit about the new shit going on now, I'd have no fucking clue. I watch my kids get into it and I love seeing them light up and just be passionate about music, but I think it's horrible. That's just how it is."

Korn probably had extra appeal to a rebellious youth market because their music wasn't largely understood or liked by everyone. *Follow The Leader* was reviewed in *Billboard* in September 1998;

Korn - *Follow The Leader*: In-depth

"With two platform albums under its belt, Korn was poised to bolt out of the gates with its latest collection, *Follow The Leader*. To make matters more attractive for Korn, the album features a collaboration with Ice Cube on 'Children Of The Korn', tapping into the hardcore rap market, as well as the band's hard rock base. Indeed, *Follow The Leader* lives up to expectations, debuting at number one on the Billboard 200 in the September 5th issue. Despite that impressive sales performance, the album offers little in the way of enduring satisfaction. Peddling industrial rock clichés and angst-ridden, often misogynistic lyrics, Korn comes across as a band without a clear purpose or an original sound. Inexplicably, the album's first twelve tracks are blank, five second cuts."

But did the album — and indeed Korn's music overall — get through to a lot of people in a way that matters in the long run? Absolutely. Head was quoted of a relatively recent day out in *The Ringer* in August 2018; "All of these people were coming up to me and saying, 'Hey man, I'm a fan of your band.' And there were African Americans coming up to me, asking for a picture. There were white people, and Hispanics. We just hit so many different types of people. Because we wanted our music to make people's heads bob."

Munky advocated in an interview on KLOS 95.5 with DJ Full Metal Jackie in June 2018 that *Follow The Leader* has been influential beyond just hard rock music; "It's crazy. All these young hip-hop kids now are coming up to me, saying, 'Man, I love your band. Because of your band, I'm into this, this and this.' And they're all these young rapper kids with tattoos all over their faces — just super hardcore. So there's a whole new movement. So it's nice for them to step up and give us an homage, I guess."

Could there be another Family Values tour around the corner? Well, Davis told *Metal Hammer* in March 2018; "Family Values could definitely happen again. I'd like to bring out trap artists and things reflecting what's going on right now in music, just like we did back in the day. There's plenty of aggressive acts in all forms of music that could tour together and do a new Family Values so it's definitely something we could look at doing again in the future."

Although controversial at times, the emotionally loaded nature of Korn's music has got through to a lot of people over the years. There's something incredibly powerful about that and it is something that Davis is very forward about. In 2019 he commented; "I think Korn's legacy will be that we helped a lot of kids deal with bullying issues, molestation issues, suicide, drug issues — that's the only reason I'm still here. To do meet and greets and see people crying saying we saved their life with a song, you can't get paid any amount of money to make you feel like that. That drives me to keep doing what I do because it touches so many people and that's what rock 'n' roll was about back in the day."

Fieldy said in *Kerrang!* in January 1999; "Every singer gets to a point where they get stuck. Novelists get writer's block. You've just got to make light of it. He's never gonna run out of feelings — he'll always have some kind of hurt in his life, even if it's more in the present than in the past... To be an emotional singer, you need to be a wreck. I hope he never becomes sane! I pick on him and try to make him cry, just so he'll have something to write about!"

Even as far back as when Korn's debut album came out, Davis often stated in interviews that he had "no idea that so many people felt the way (he) felt."

When asked to expand upon what that experience was like for him, he told *Kerrang!* in May 2018; "It made me feel not so alone, but sad that a lot of people were going through the sorrow that I went through. You come to the realisation as you get older that life is not easy, no matter what you're doing. I'm living my fucking childhood dream, but there are consequences. People say to me, 'You're a big, bad rockstar who's rich, you don't have anything to worry about.' I have to grit my teeth and smile, because I've got more shit to fucking worry about. With every great thing there's an equally bad thing that's going to happen. That's how the universe works."

No matter what Korn do musically, it is never without emotional honesty. In response to the question of "Do you never want to forget about all your problems and not talk or sing about them?", Davis replied; "No, because I tried that all my life and it didn't get me nowhere. It's better for me to scream about 'em."

Head told *Loudwire* in September 2019; "Jonathan really uses his lyrics and writing records as therapy for himself. It's like he processes his pain with music and creativity."

Davis retorted; "I go on tour and get an opportunity to vent what I'm feeling. It's always been my refuge, my escape, my church. Some people go get a shrink, I've got my music. I wish sometimes I was born back in the day because today's society is just so fucked up. Now it's just ridiculous. When I write, I think about how a lot of people are in the closet about their thoughts. That's a shame. They should at least talk about the bad things going on, and don't act on it. Don't keep it all inside, so when you explode you actually do something bad. It's like, get it out. My writing is my venting process."

Upon being asked whether he ever felt the need to lighten up the lyrics, Davis said to *New Musical Express* in September 1998; "All our albums have been pretty grim, that's what inspires me. Shit, I don't feel right singing about happy shit."

There is something endearing about artists being unapologetic in embracing their emotions and indeed, their quirks — even if they're a bit on the sinister side. Davis told *New Musical Express* in 2019; "I've just always been drawn to the dark stuff. As I've got older I've started to understand the importance of balance. My house, which is full of some fucking crazy dark things — is actually quite a peaceful place. People always say that when they come to visit. There's a good balance between light and dark. For me, peace is that fine line between the two. But I can't deny that I haven't always been fascinated by really dark things, although as a person I think I come from a place of light. I'm kind, I'm not mean or cruel, I want to help people... Dude, I've been seeing ghosts since I was a little fucking child. I believe. I totally believe."

Fieldy said in *Kerrang!* in January 1999; "No matter what we do, it's always gonna be heavy and dark. You're always going to know it's Korn, because I think we've established our sound."

Overall, Korn were incredibly influential. Even today, you would be hard pressed to find a band that look and sound like Korn. Whilst others might try, there's still only one Korn. And rightly so. *Follow The Leader* is iconic, original and worth a listen. It was then and it is now — over twenty years since its release. Davis said in

2018; "It feels fucking good, to get that respect. I walk in the room with younger bands and they're like, 'Holy fucking shit!' I remember that feeling, like when we got our first gold record from Ozzy. Now that we've stood the test of time, I ain't gonna lie: It's fucking dope."

Korn - *Follow The Leader*: In-depth

A Comprehensive Discography

Personnel

Korn
Jonathan Davis — vocals, bagpipes
Head — electric guitar
Munky — electric guitar
Fieldy — bass guitar
David Silveria — drums, percussion

Additional Vocalists
Fred Durst — on 'All In The Family'
Tre Hardson — on 'Cameltosis'
Ice Cube — on 'Children Of The Korn'
Cheech Marin — on 'Earache My Eye'

Production Staff
Todd McFarlane and Greg Capullo — artwork
Brian Haberlin — artwork (colouring)
Joseph Cultice — photography
Tommy D. Daugherty — programming
John Ewing, Jr. — engineer, assistant engineer
Ross Robinson - vocal coaching
Stephen Marcussen — mastering
Brendan O'Brien — mixing
Steve Thompson — producer
Don C. Tyler — digital editing
Justin Z. Walden — additional drums, programming
Toby Wright — producer, engineer

Track Listing

1. It's On! (4:28)
2. Freak on a Leash (4:15)
3. Got The Life (3:45)
4. Dead Bodies Everywhere (4:44)
5. Children of the Korn (featuring Ice Cube) (3:52)
6. B.B.K. (3:56)
7. Pretty (4:12)
8. All In The Family (featuring Fred Durst) (4:48)
9. Reclaim My Place (4:32)
10. Justin (4:17)
11. Seed (5:54)
12. Cameltosis (featuring Tre Hardson) (4:38)
13. My Gift To You (My Gift To You ends at 7:12. A hidden track entitled Earache My Eye, a Cheech & Chong cover, starts at 9:12, after 2 minutes of silence) (15:40)

The original CD release features twenty-five tracks. The album starts with twelve hidden tracks consisting of five seconds of silence each, totaling sixty seconds of silence, with 'It's On!' starting on track thirteen.

US/UK discography variations

Original US releases:
Immortal Records EK 69001, CD, 18th August 1998
Immortal Records E2 69001, LP, 18th August 1998
Immortal Records ET69001, cassette, 18th August 1998

US reissues:
Immortal Records 88875121211, 2LP, 2015
_{1000 copies pressed. Clear vinyl. Machine-numbered in gold ink on back cover.}
Immortal Records 19075865851, 2LP, 17th August 2018
_{20th Anniversary Gold Vinyl. Limited to 2000 units.}
Immortal Records 190758658513, 2LP, 7th September 2018
_{Korn webstore exclusive 20th anniversary red vinyl edition of 750.}
Immortal Records 19075865851, 2LP, 7th September 2018

Original UK releases:
Epic EPC 491221 2, CD, 1998
Epic, QUORNBX1, 3CD, 1998
_{Limited Edition box set of 2,000 copies with 2 CD singles, stickers and T-shirt.}
Epic – EPC 491221 9, 2CD, 1998
_{Special limited edition 2CD, includes exclusive remixes by DJ Clark Kent, Level X and Scarecrow}

UK reissues:
Epic 88697101852, CD, 2007
Epic MOVLP667, 2LP, 15th September 2014
_{Limited Edition, 2000 individually numbered copies, gold vinyl.}
Epic 19075865851, 2LP, 17th August 2018

Tour Dates

Lollapalooza Tour 1997

Wednesday 25th June	Coral Sky Amphitheatre, West Palm Beach, FL, USA
Friday 27th June	Lakewood Amphitheatre, Atlanta, GA, USA
Saturday 28th June	Blockbuster Pavilion, Charlotte, NC, USA
Sunday 29th June	Hardee's Walnut Creek Amphitheatre, Raleigh, NC, USA
Tuesday 1st July	GTE Amphitheatre, Virginia Beach, VA, USA
Wednesday 2nd July	Nissan Pavilion, Bristow, VA, USA
Friday 4th July	Kingswood Music Theatre, Vaughan, ON, Canada
Saturday 5th July	Darien Lake Performing Arts Centre, Darien Centre, NY, USA
Tuesday 8th July	Great Woods Amphitheatre, Mansfield, MA, USA
Friday 11th July	Downing Stadium, New York, NY, USA
Saturday 12th July	Blockbuster-Sony Music Entertainment Centre, Camden, NJ, USA
Sunday 13th July	Meadows Music Theatre, Hartford, CT, USA
Tuesday 15th July	Pine Knob Music Theatre, Clarkston, MI, USA
Wednesday 16th July	Pine Knob Music Theatre, Clarkston, MI, USA
Friday 18th July	Blossom Music Centre, Cuyahoga Falls, OH, USA
Saturday 19th July	Coca-Cola Star Lake Amphitheatre, Burgettstown, PA, USA

Korn had to cancel their scheduled appearances at the following Lollapalooza shows due to Munky taking ill...

Sunday 20th July	Polaris Amphitheatre, Columbus, OH, USA
Tuesday 22nd July	Riverbend Music Centre, Cincinnati, OH, USA
Wednesday 23rd July	Deer Creek Music Centre, Noblesville, IN, USA
Friday 25th July	New World Music Theatre, Tinley Park, IL, USA
Saturday 26th July	Val-Du-Lakes Amphitheatre, Mears, MI, USA
Sunday 27th July	Alpine Valley Music Theatre, East Troy, WI, USA
Tuesday 29th July	Sandstone Amphitheatre, Bonner Springs, KS, USA
Wednesday 30th July	Riverport Amphitheatre, St. Louis, MO, USA
Thursday 30th July	Starwood Amphitheatre, Antioch, TN, USA
Saturday 2nd August	Starplex Amphitheatre, Dallas, TX, USA
Sunday 3rd August	Texas Sky Park, Corpus Christi, TX, USA
Wednesday 6th August	Desert Sky Pavilion, Phoenix, AZ, USA
Friday 8th August	Blockbuster Pavilion, San Bernardino, CA, USA
Sunday 10th August	Fiddler's Green Amphitheatre, Greenwood Village, CO, USA
Tuesday 12th August	The Gorge Amphitheatre, George, WA, USA
Wednesday 13th August	Portland Meadows, Portland, OR, USA
Friday 15th August	Concord Pavilion, Concord, CA, USA
Saturday 16th August	Shoreline Amphitheatre, Mountain View, CA, USA

The final date of the year did take place:

Saturday 13th December	Milan, Italy

1998

Saturday 20th June   Ozzfest Milton Keynes National Bowl, Milton Keynes, England *Cancelled*.
Sunday 2nd August   Fuji Rock Festival, Toyosu Bay-side Square, Tokyo, Japan
Tuesday 25th August   Family Values Kampaign 98, Philadelphia, PA, USA

Family Values Tour 1998

Tuesday 22nd September	Blue Cross Arena, Rochester, NY, USA
Wednesday 23rd September	Worcester's Centrum Centre, Worcester, MA, USA
Friday 25th September	Continental Airlines Arena, East Rutherford, NJ, USA
Saturday 26th September	First Union Spectrum, Philadelphia, PA, USA
Sunday 27th September	CSU Convocation Centre, Cleveland, OH, USA
Tuesday 29th September	Civic Arena, Pittsburgh, PA, USA
Wednesday 30th September	The Palace of Auburn Hills, Auburn Hills, MI, USA
Friday 2nd October	Wisconsin Centre Arena, Milwaukee, WI, USA
Saturday 3rd October	Rosemont Horizon, Rosemont, IL, USA
Sunday 4th October	Target Centre, Minneapolis, MN, USA
Tuesday 6th October	McNichols Sports Arena, Denver, CO, USA
Friday 9th October	Great Western Forum, Inglewood, CA, USA
Saturday 10th October	Cow Palace, Daly City, CA, USA
Sunday 11th October	Thomas & Mack Centre, Las Vegas, NV, USA
Monday 12th October	America West Arena, Phoenix, AZ, USA
Tuesday 13th October	Idaho Centre, Boise, ID, USA *Cancelled*.
Wednesday 14th October	E Centre, West Valley, UT, USA
Friday 16th October	Fort Worth Convention Centre, Fort Worth, TX, USA
Saturday 17th October	Cajundome, Lafayette, LA, USA
Sunday 18th October	Kiefer UNO Lakefront Arena, New Orleans, LA, USA

Most of the footage on the Family Values Video and CD was captured at this show.

Tuesday 20th October	Fairgrounds Arena, Oklahoma City, OK, USA
Thursday 22nd October	Kemper Arena, Kansas City, MO, USA
Friday 23rd October	Keil Centre, St. Louis, MO, USA
Saturday 24th October	Omaha Civic Auditorium, Omaha, NE, USA
Monday 26th October	Wings Stadium, Kalamazoo, MI, USA
Tuesday 27th October	Market Square Arena, Indianapolis, IN, USA
Thursday 29th October	New Haven Veterans Memorial Coliseum, New Haven, CT, USA
Friday 30th October	Nassau Veterans Memorial Coliseum, Uniondale, NY, USA
Saturday 31st October	Patriot Centre, Fairfax, VA, USA
Monday 2nd November	Arrow Hall, Mississauga, ON, Canada
Tuesday 3rd November	Universite de Montreal CEPSUM, Montreal, QC, Canada
Wednesday 4th November	RPI Fieldhouse, Troy, NY, USA CANCELLED
Friday 6th November	Mullins Centre, Amherst, MA, USA
Saturday 7th November	Tsongas Arena, Lowell, MA, USA
Sunday 8th November	Cumberland County Civic Centre, Portland, ME, USA
Tuesday 10th November	Hampton Coliseum, Hampton, VA, USA
Wednesday 11th November	Independence Arena, Charlotte, NC, USA
Friday 13th November	Lakeland Centre, Lakeland, FL, USA
Saturday 14th November	Bayfront Park Amphitheatre, Miami, FL, USA
Monday 16th November	International Ballroom, Atlanta, GA, USA
Tuesday 17th November	Knoxville Civic Coliseum, Knoxville, TN, USA

Thursday 19th November	Astroarena, Houston, TX, USA
Friday 20th November	Mid-South Coliseum, Memphis, TN, USA
Saturday 21st November	Nashville Municipal Auditorium, Nashville, TN, USA
Friday 11th December	Shrine Auditorium, Los Angeles, CA, USA
	KROQ Almost Acoustic Christmas

Big Day Out '99

Friday 15th January	Ericsson Stadium, Auckland, New Zealand
Sunday 17th January	Gold Coast Parklands, Gold Coast, Australia
Saturday 23rd January	Olympic Park, Sydney, Australia
Tuesday 26th January	Royal Melbourne Showgrounds, Melbourne, Australia
Friday 29th January	Royal Adelaide Showgrounds, Adelaide, Australia
Sunday 31st January	Bassendean Oval, Perth, Australia

Japanese Tour

Thursday 4th February	Zepp Osaka, Osaka, Japan
Friday 5th February	Tokyo Bay NK Hall, Chiba, Japan
Saturday 6th February	Tokyo Bay NK Hall, Chiba, Japan

Rock Is Dead Tour

Friday 26th February	Tucson Convention Centre, Tucson, AZ, USA
Saturday 27th February	Tingley Coliseum, Albuquerque, NM, USA
Sunday 28th February	El Paso County Coliseum, El Paso, TX, USA
Tuesday 2nd March	Freeman Coliseum, San Antonio, TX, USA
Wednesday 3rd March	Reunion Arena, Dallas, TX, USA
Friday 5th March	Mississippi Coast Coliseum, Biloxi, MS, USA
Saturday 6th March	Times-Union Centre for the Performing Arts, Jacksonville, FL, USA
Sunday 7th March	Ice Palace, Tampa, FL, USA
Tuesday 9th March	National Car Rental Centre, Sunrise, FL, USA
Thursday 11th March	Ervin J. Nutter Centre, Fairborn, OH, USA
Friday 12th March	Mark of the Quad Cities, Moline, IL, USA
Saturday 13th March	The Palace of Auburn Hills, Auburn Hills, MI, USA
Monday 15th March	Copps Coliseum, Hamilton, ON, Canada
Tuesday 16th March	Toledo Sports Arena, Toledo, OH, USA
Thursday 18th March	Broome County Veterans Memorial Arena, Binghamton, NY, USA
Friday 19th March	Worcester's Centrum Centre, Worcester, MA, USA
Saturday 20th March	Providence Civic Centre, Providence, RI, USA
Monday 22nd March	Bryce Jordan Centre, University Park, PA, USA
Tuesday 23rd March	First Union Centre, Philadelphia, PA, USA
Thursday 25th March	Rosemont Horizon, Rosemont, IL, USA
Friday 26th March	Allen County War Memorial Coliseum, Fort Wayne, IN, USA
Saturday 27th March	Van Andel Arena, Grand Rapids, MI, USA
Monday 19th March	Greensboro Coliseum, Greensboro, NC, USA
Tuesday 30th March	BI-LO Centre, Greenville, SC, USA
Thursday 1st April	Louisville Gardens, Louisville, KY, USA

Friday 2nd April	BJCC Arena, Birmingham, AL, USA
Saturday 3rd April	Barton Coliseum, Little Rock, AR, USA
Monday 5th April	Dane County Coliseum, Madison, WI, USA
Tuesday 6th April	Fargodome, Fargo, ND, USA
Friday 9th April	Tacoma Dome, Tacoma, WA, USA
Saturday 10th April	Portland Memorial Coliseum, Portland, OR, USA
Monday 12th April	ARCO Arena, Sacramento, CA, USA
Tuesday 13th April	The Arena in Oakland, Oakland, CA, USA
Wednesday 14th April	Bakersfield Centennial Garden, Bakersfield, CA, USA
Friday 16th April	Arrowhead Pond, Anaheim, CA, USA
Saturday 17th April	Cox Arena, San Diego, CA, USA
Sunday 18th April	Blockbuster Pavilion, San Bernardino, CA, USA
Tuesday 20th April	Arizona Veterans Memorial Coliseum, Phoenix, AZ, USA
Thursday 22nd April	Kansas Coliseum, Valley Centre, KS, USA
Friday 23rd April	Kemper Arena, Kansas City, MO, USA
Tuesday 20th July	Whisky A Go Go, West Hollywood, CA, USA
Friday 23rd July	Woodstock '99, Griffiss Air Force Base, Rome, NY, USA

Family Values Tour '99

Tuesday 5th October	Van Andel Arena, Grand Rapids, MI, USA
Wednesday 6th October	Market Square Arena, Indianapolis, IN, USA
Friday 8th October	Value City Arena At The Schottenstein Centre, Columbus, OH, USA
Saturday 9th October	Allstate Arena, Rosemont, IL, USA
Sunday 10th October	Kiel Centre, St. Louis, MO, USA
Tuesday 12th October	Kemper Arena, Kansas City, MO, USA
Wednesday 13th October	Target Centre, Minneapolis, MN, USA
Monday 15th November	Apollo Theatre, New York, NY, USA

****Tuesday 16th November *Issues* is released****

In-depth Series

The In-depth series was launched in March 2021 with four titles. Each book takes an in-depth look at an album; the history behind it; the story about its creation; the songs, as well as detailed discographies listing release variations around the world. The series will tackle albums that are considered to be classics amongst the fan bases, as well as some albums deemed to be "difficult" or controversial; shining new light on them, following reappraisal by the authors.

Titles to date:

Jethro Tull - Thick As A Brick	*978-1-912782-57-4*
Tears For Fears - The Hurting	*978-1-912782-58-1*
Kate Bush - The Kick Inside	*978-1-912782-59-8*
Deep Purple - Stormbringer	*978-1-912782-60-4*
Emerson Lake & Palmer - Pictures At An Exhibition	978-1-912782-67-3
Korn - Follow The Leader	978-1-912782-68-0
Elvis Costello - This Year's Model	978-1-912782-69-7
Kate Bush - The Dreaming	978-1-912782-70-3

Forthcoming:

Jethro Tull - Minstrel In The Gallery	978-1-912782-81-9
Deep Purple - Fireball	978-1-912782-82-6
Deep Purple - Slaves And Masters	978-1-912782-83-3
Talking Heads - Remain In Light	
Jethro Tull - Heavy Horses	
Rainbow - Straight Between The Eyes	
The Stranglers - La Folie	
Alice Cooper - Love It To Death	